When someone asks what there is to do,
Light the candle in his hand.

Like this.

—Jalal ad-Din Rumi

"In the beginning were the instructions. We were to have compassion for one another, to live and work together, to depend on each other for support. We were told we were all related and interconnected to each other."

Tesuque Pueblo Elder

Legendary

A TRIBUTE TO THOSE WHO
HONORABLY SERVE DEVALUED CHILDREN

Dear Laura

Legendary

A TRIBUTE TO THOSE WHO
HONORABLY SERVE DEVALUED CHILDREN

Jaiya John

Your Soul Sings in Lyrics of Light!

SWR
Soul Water Rising

Ojai, California

Love Jaiya

1.15.15

Legendary: A Tribute to Those Who Honorably Serve Devalued Children

Copyright © 2014 by Jaiya John

Printed in the United States of America

Soul Water Rising
Ojai, California
http://www.soulwater.org

Library of Congress Control Number: 2014908369
ISBN 978-0-9916401-0-2

Second Soul Water Rising Edition, Softcover: 2014

Poetry / Child Welfare, Social Services, and Education

Editors:
Jacqueline V. Richmond
Kent W. Mortensen

Jacket and Interior Design: Jaiya John
Jacket Photo © 2010 by Jaiya John

Look at that young cat
singin' the blues.

He's not complaining,
just exclaiming:

My pain has a purpose,
like splinters in the pews.

I'm deeper cause
I've been to the deepness.

My journey brings good news.

Now, put down your troubles,
and help me to sing these blues.

—Jaiya John

AUTHOR'S NOTE

She must have been only in her forties. Thick locks of hair falling over cavernous eyes. Those eyes. Pools of emotion overflowing their banks, dropping tears into the lagoon of my compassion. Leaning over the table, she took my hand and said to me in a determined voice, "Thank you for giving me the strength to carry on. You reminded me why I do this work. And why not everyone does. Honestly, I have felt burned out and weary. I was considering a change of careers. Thank you, just for understanding."

Such moments have occurred hundreds of times in brief intimate moments of honesty I have been blessed to share with people during my speaking engagements and in correspondence. A great majority of my audiences are teachers, social workers, counselors, advocates, mentors, and the like. So often they serve children and youth who have been devalued by a demanding society. A culture that assigns worth to our young based on social norms.

When our young do not meet those norms, they suffer the ransacking assault of daily derogation that pillages self-Love from their very breast. These are youth who have committed the *offenses* of being materially impoverished; separated from family; homeless; or challenged in learning, behavior, mental health, or physical ability. Or they have *sinned* due to their heritage, language, or trauma from abuse or neglect. They are a collective aching heart and their numbers are massive.

This book, these poems and poetic stories, are for those who honorably serve our devalued young. They honor not because of their vocation, but because of the spirit in which they conduct their service. Their personal ethic will not let them betray the often hard truth of what must be done for a child. Their vision penetrates the sometimes illusory surface persona of youth to see the beauty and promise that live within. They summon the courage to reckon with their prejudices, shed their egos, and release their own greatness. A true teacher is in fact a social worker, given to the task of cultivating through children our collective social well-being. A true social worker is certainly a teacher, daring enough to enlighten both youth and colleague, according to not what is popular, but what is essential.

All who serve in this manner have earned the high title of being both teacher and social worker. They tend a sacred garden of youthfulness. We must elevate their name. They are underpaid and uncelebrated by our culture. We ask the world of them but provide slight and fickle support as they toil against youthful struggle in all its enormity. They are not celebrities, athletes, or tycoons. Yet their brave, enduring devotion truly lives on in the immeasurable ripple of goodness that feeds generations. My prayer is that such servants will drink from these words and be filled.

DEAR CARING ONE

Dear One Who Cares Enough to Serve My Life:

I am a child for now. One day I will be the cascading consequence of your touch. Last night in my room, I found myself releasing a watershed's gathering of tears. I fell asleep as a river. When I woke I realized what that river was: a flow of gratitude. For you.

Dear Caring One... If ever you find yourself as a river filled with too much... just, *too much*... I hope you will take out my words, and swallow them into your heart, so you will know that who you are is always Greater than what sometimes feels like *just too much*. I want you to know I am a river that passed once by you, and when I arrived, you did not turn away. *You did not turn away.*

The first time you sat with me, you chose to look from your soul into mine. I could see you *seeing me*. I could feel you *feeling me*. In that moment I had found an island on which to rest my weariness in this wide and unforgiving sea. You let me glimpse just a little evidence of your own life struggles in the honest quiver of your face. In spirit, I felt you take my hand and join me in this deserted place they call *The Young Who Is In Need.*

I wonder when they will realize that when my heart is cut, it is the entire human soul that bleeds.

You told me secret stories of your scars, and fears, and doubts, and how your own tender blossom was violated before you ever released your bloom. You watched over me with Love, even as society watched over you, suspicious of us both. Each time they wanted to brand me with stigmatic lies and cast me to the dungeon of social banishment, your voice cried out: *This life will not be left to scavengers. Its sun will surely shine!*

I began to know what hope feels like, as you showed me how your life's fate was hitched to mine. Over and over in panic I drew my weapon of distrust against your advances. Instead of gunning me down in return by giving up on me, you smiled and said: *Holster your fear, and come inside the shelter of your possibilities.* I did. You stood at the door, on guard while I lay down to catch a rare and needed sleep.

When I woke, you were there, with bowls full of fresh hot faith in me, and lightness and laughter poured in cups of tea. You ate with me. Which is to say: You wrapped your human soul around my human struggle and let me feel your heat. You were going to care enough for me to do whatever it took. I know that look. I've seen it in the eyes of parents well enough to protect their young, and halt the world at the line of indiscretion against their offspring.

I keep springing off from earth on forays of fantasy, looking for an escape from my reality. You keep risking merciless outer space, with no fancy ship or special suit, to bring me back to the planet of my destiny. You help me to see that what I thought was my reality is my illusion, and that I can arrange the stones of my circumstance into a staircase ascending into the life I dream.

Do you know how great you are? You stand your ground every time I scream. I walk heavy... you lift me up in laughter. When laws and rules say: *No, we can't do that to help that one,* you crush that *No* under your heel and by force of will give *No* no choice but to turn into a *Yes.* You change laws and rules by the power of your devotion. You change this world. For caring is revolution's greatest sword and you wield that gleaming power. You are the sixty strokes of endurance that help pass my fateful hour.

When I fear sunset, you lift the disbelieving sun for just a while longer. When I falter, you alter my course with kind correction and firm resolve. When I thirst, you pour more water. In my darkness, here comes your candlelight. You teach me by the way you touch me how to kindly touch our humankind.

I carry a porous bag leaking my relationships. You walk behind with your brave basin catching all the drops. I have never heard you slur my mom or curse my pops. Never sensed you insinuate that I come from *bad people*, or that *good people* will save my life. Your lesson is always about the goodness inside what looks like badness, and that I, like the earth, and being *of the earth*, carry all that I need to heal myself, reveal myself, kneel myself down before my Greatness and let life's cleansing breath carry all my woundedness away.

On this day, Dear Caring One, I hope my words infiltrate your fatigue. That my words live inside you, a Love virus you can never eradicate. This world and its values cannot measure you. Only the lives you touch can do that. Cruelness and coldness can never create new life. Only your Light can do that. The Peace you so deserve is pronounced *compassion*. This Peace sits waiting in old oak barrels only your Love can tap.

Dear Caring One, lift my words to your lips and drink this truth into your heart: You are the Greatest Gift this young life has ever known. If I am royalty, your service is my throne.

In Gratitude Forever,

A child for now... One day, the full grown life that your Loving honed.

YOUR SACRED CALLING

Dear Soul Servant, Sacred Warrior, Healer, Teacher, Compassionate One...

If you work in good faith to serve the tender land of childhood, then you, my friend, stand at the center of this ceremony.

If you hold in your heart a Sacred place, purified with sweet grass and cedar, that ill spirit cannot touch, then you, my sister, brother, are one of the Carriers of Light.

If a fire burns in you to see suffering cease; if you cry tears of Love at the sight of Beauty; if you can feel in the silence between these words the Dream Song, the Earth Medicine, the Sky Vision, the Water Dance, the Ancestral Drum that our human journey is weaving as a warm blanket of sweet grass against the cold, then you, my kin, sit around an ancient fire, even if you have forgotten the warmth of its touch.

A fire that depends on us gathering soulful wood so that it may continue burning, and our circle may go unbroken.

And you should know this:

We, the ones who swim where the water is deep, Bow Down to your Grace, lift up our eyes to your Glory, and Celebrate your Servitude. Your sweet breath is the morning dew and mountain mist

giving suffering souls Hope that somewhere in
this world... Someone cares. And that a new day
will dawn in the end.

Namasté.

COMPASSION'S LIGHT

She speaks to her graduating class
of social work students
with a melancholy heart,

for she has come to Love them,
they in their bright plumage of anticipation,
clamoring for change.

She knows that from the first moment
these missionaries step into human lives,
they will be touched in ways profound.

It is they who will be changed.

Her message is a tender plucking of strings,
a Spanish guitar ballad before eager dancers,

a serenade:

Ours is a unique path.
We are flagpoles for social justice.
We acknowledge injustice.

We insert social duty to the vulnerable

into a conversation enamored
with power and wealth.

We advocate for change,
empower the masses to address
the injustices heaped on their souls.

We identify with the oppressed.

This is not a mind game
or trickery of association.

We dig deep and discover that we *are* the
oppressed. They are a physical extension
of our own existence.

We appear to stand as plants distinct from them,
occupying different plots of the garden,

yet ultimately, our roots grow from the same
ground, are nourished and poisoned
by the same soil.

We inhabit the same garden,
breathe the same air.

What ails the oppressed will reach us in time.
Our neglect of inequity returns to us magnified.

Identifying with indigent lives
is no cute condescension.

It is the hard realization
that our physical body serves

as no boundary at all
when despair chooses to crawl.

If we do not care for the least and distant,
we endanger our most beLoved.

This world a flood plain
for all that we allow to be.

We plant dignity and worth in the same ground
that arrogance plants its acid seed.

Where the world plants salt and lye,
we plant richness and lime.

Human relations make the world barren.
Human relations can make barrenness a paradise.

Integrity is a hard coin to find
on the streets of hedonism,
yet we search for its shine
in gutters and drains,
holding fast to excellence
in flood tides of mediocrity.

Territorial temptations lead us
into phantom kingdoms where
we believe we rule the land,

but in time our possessiveness
strangles the vines.

We wake up cold and chilled in the night
to discover that we rule nothing but
dust mites and weeds.

All souls desert a territory possessed.

No place is worse than a troll-patrolled house.
Nothing grows in kingdoms ruled by a mouse.

The modest serve greatly,
the blowhards blow harder,
but lose at the barter
between greatness and shame.

Downtrodden lose at the game,
but their day, too, comes
when the tables have turned,

and who was rich in pocket
but poor in the heart,
finds all that was valued
has crumpled and burned,

and all that was despised,
has grown through the cries
to become rich in the soul
and favored by the skies.

We who walk this road
must never stop learning,
for the dark cloud of ignorance
never stops burning,

and we must be faithful,
for how can we teach our children to hope
unless we believe that change
is ever a possible and ordained thing.

History looks favorably on she
who gives her life to humanity.

Its scrolls carry the tale of honorable
servants with the gift of many tongues,

able to speak and decipher
the myriad languages of
suffering and promise.

Children howl in a special code.
Citizens react as if knowing what
they are trying to communicate.

Yet they have not bothered
to decipher the neophyte language.

But we have.

And we must be honest,
for comfortable lives often build
fortresses constructed of lies.

But pain blisters the paint on such walls,
leaving the broken homeless indeed.

Only honesty builds character
that passes the muster.

So walk through the veil of pain,
bless yourself with all it reveals.
Your purpose lies beyond the veil.

My students,
we must be role models of compassion,
for the world's faculty is fat with instructors
who write cold lesson plans.

Do not look for leadership into a better world.
Become that leadership.

Move the world.

WHAT BECOMES OF A SCHOOLHOUSE

The coach and the preacher
meet with the teacher.
Together they draft a declaration:

What happens to a school house
whose souls have been stolen?

What of the teeters that don't totter,
the swings lonesome for bottoms to bear?

The playground once so fancy,
now strident and *safe,*
its grass gone to dust?

We don't mean to make a fuss
and yet we must. We must.

We hear no squeaking of shoes
on the gym floor, as we used to.

Administration exclaims the high liability
of children who run.

What of their bodies that never see sun?
What of their bellies swollen on sugar,
their arteries gathering their plaque,
by age 40 the coming of their
non-liable heart attack?

The hallways are dreary,
which should not surprise us.
After all, music was banished so long ago,

just after colors were bleached from bleachers,
and up went the barbed wire fences and walls.

*We have to teach them the basics
or we'll fail them,* THEY say.

What of the failure of Joy
given no time to play?

What of the clouds children
used to daydream about?

What of their doodles and impromptu games?
Their jokes and their riddles and shouting of
names?

Did you enjoy school today?
their parents ask, so hopeful.

But with no double dutch
no hopscotch, jacks, or jump rope,

where is the laughter,
the magic,
the reason for hope?

What becomes of a schoolhouse
where soul does not dwell?

When does the wind blow that lifts morose spell
and gives learning a chance to be Loved?

We build more schools and more prisons, too.
In both places, we sanitize away all truth.

Truth is not tidy or easy to predict.
It smudges and grudges and speaks out of line.
it stumbles and fumbles and throws quite the fit.

Truth is a young life allowed to encounter
its cry, dance, and holler.

Growing stalks need to touch one another
so as to confirm their growth.

Dubious shepherds with wicked sticks
seek to tame this growth
by cutting down novice candlewick.

Earth has always born those who teach
by incarcerating,
forcing children to learn by peeking through bars.

We seek new script:
pedagogy through humility,
learning through boldness and lucidity.

We ask once again,
what becomes of a schoolyard
with no living things?

We have made a decision:
We will no longer participate in any demolition
of our young.

From this day forward, we demand that children
be allowed to leave their human fingerprints

everywhere.

On everything.

HONOR THIS CHILD

Hardly anyone is in the courtroom this day
as she stands up to advocate for a life whose fate
depends on whose voice will be strongest.

The willful judge is about to decree
when she, the advocate,
says:

Your Honor,
this child...

Your...
honor this child

What did you say?

I said, honor this child.

With all due respect, judge,
you will not place him in a home
where prejudice toward his very being
gnaws at his self-Love like rats
hidden in the walls
that visit him at night.

You will not banish him to a program
that conceives of him as inherently flawed,

as an ill-mixed clay fit only for pounding
on the table by angry hands.

I will not go home tonight having stood here
and allowed this child to be dispersed
according to the law's discretion,
when no one has previously shown
any just discretion in his unattended life.

I will not go home and eat my dinner
and tuck in my children
and sleep sweet dreams.

I will not return to the office tomorrow
and be greeted kindly by colleagues
as we collaborate with a *system*
on mediocre intervention
in frightfully troubled lives,

or fail to intervene at all.

I will not keep closed my mouth
as you render your judgment
as though finality has been passed.

No child's life should ever be cast
in such abbreviated possibility.

Every single such life deserves and demands
the fullest amendments to its story
until we have arrived at a suitable plot
not concluding with a graveyard of desolation.

Hammer your gavel with all your might.
Find me in contempt, because I am.

I have contempt for this parade
of excuse and rationale.

I have contempt for our blaring trumpets
of self-congratulation.

I have utter contempt for our acceptance
of less than our best for *other people's children.*

if not me,
then who will stand up against hurtful laws?
Who will risk losing his job
so a child won't lose her life?

I will.
I will lose my job, and take my scolding,
but I will walk out of this courtroom
a human being who bent not before might.

This child will see wrong turned to right
before you or I greet our goodnight.

so, your honor,
honor this child.

EARMARK THIS CHILD

Standing before congress, the worker testifies:

Ladies and gentlemen, as you appropriate,
please remember:

This child is not a grant, a request for proposal,
a 10-year-study, a strategic plan,
a child-centered, community-based,
culturally-competent rhetoric.

This child is now, immediate, true,
touched by plague of our own hollowness.

We must serve this child, now.

This child is *not* a category, diagnosis,
prediction, predicament, case,
acronym for sin or surrender.

Is *not* a test score, performance, grade,
pie chart, bar graph, point on the bell curve,
outlier, mean, median or mode.

Is *not* cattle for prodding onto a life track
and fattened with self-doubt for slaughter.

Is *not* a quota of outcomes,
a trigger for funding renewal.

This child is a banged up knee,
a story still being written much less told.

A footprint on Earth,
a song in the wind,

a blessing in the world,
an anger at the mouth of our failure's cave.

Sorrow of a slave,
revolt of servitude,
uprising of dignity.

A bloodied lip,
a sassy input,

a reminder, a warning,
a beacon, a borrowed thing.

A litmus, an escapee from our *promises*,
a signpost, indication, night light,
goose talk, North Star.

Reason, season, hope,
checkmate on our spiritual board.

This child is our absolute
and final frontier.

We had better earmark
this young life as though it were
pumping oil out of its little heart
enough to satisfy our greed

forever.

MINNOWS AND FROGS

At the staff meeting,
the workers discuss their various
roles and responsibilities.

Midway through, one worker interrupts
with a pensive voice:

We have neglected a priority item,
failed to even include it on our agenda.
The subject we must address
is that of our collective responsibility.

I need no planner, scheduler, pen or pad
to write this down amongst my many tasks.

I need a heart, a mind, a reason, the truth.
I require faith and determination.

Our responsibility is the child.
Our role is to serve the child.

We have *one* responsibility.

One role.

Our job descriptions, titles, positions
are secondary.

In many ways they are illusion
in this great and singular task.

We are all vulnerable, needful,
dependent souls tethered to each other.

We are wet and soaking
in the same stream.

The side stream of devalued
human beings.

I would like to share a story.

I left this little boy
a quick note on blue paper.

It said:

Before you were ever judged
by a person on this planet,
you were judged to be
beautiful and worthy of life.

The breath of life itself
was your entrance ticket,
your stamp into the club.

You were born worthy.
You already passed your greatest test.

Something Great thought you priceless
enough to be created.

The rest of your life is not an audition,
it is a grand performance.

You have already been chosen
to grace the stage.

Now, dance, sing,
make your point to the world.

We are not your director.
We are your audience.
Greatness Itself directs you.
We can only witness and learn.

I saw him tuck the note
in his pants pocket.

I prayed it would not get
washed in the laundry.

Slowly,
his demeanor changed
the remainder of the school year.

On the last day of class,
he tugged at my arm,
said he needed to talk to me.

Outside, on the main entrance steps,
he shared his secret with me, saying:

It has not been easy for me being in this place.

All of you adults have different titles,
which seems to make you pull on us
students in competing ways.

You each take a chunk out of me daily
to feed your sense of control.

I feel like a minnow pulled to pieces
by frogs who will not leave their lily pads
to join me in the water.

I keep thinking that if they did join me,
they could feel what it is like
for a minnow like me.

When you gave me that note,
I did nothing with it at first.

I thought you were just another frog
preying on me with a note for a tongue.

Eventually, I opened up the note.
I read it, and instantly I felt safer here
in this place where *you are,*

not a predatory thing,
but a big minnow
who actually wants to swim with me.

I wish all the adults here would forget
their roles and titles
and remember me.

PERMANENT TOUCH

At the podium,
on the stage,
in the late evening of her retirement party,

she graciously receives the applause
of family, friends, colleagues, and
students, present and past.

Her eyes still twinkle
after all the years.

She speaks into the microphone:

Tonight I wish to tell the truth.

So much of this work we do
in caring for our children
becomes tainted with the lies we tell ourselves
so that we may retain a measure of dignity.

Tonight, as you honor me,
I feel it is only right that I honor
the truth of what I have been,

so that who comes after me
might dare to attain a higher service.

About midway through my career,
a boy showed up in my class
about a week after fall term began.

He wore blue shoes.

His clothes smelled of urine each day.
His hair was a matted mess.

His breath stank, his skin was ashy.
He was shy, quiet, withdrawn.

Each class subject I taught,
he spent with his head down,
drawing in his notebook.

He ate his lunch alone in the cafeteria.
The other children were not so much
mean to him as thoroughly uninterested.

His build was lithe, emaciated.
He ate little, always mumbling to himself
as he finished his food.

I was concerned about this boy.
My calls to his mother went unreturned.

He walked to and from school,
so I never saw her pick him up.

Though I did not have to,
the truth is,
I chose to conclude many things about this boy.

Finally, I decided to visit his home.
His mother invited me in.

I sat on a sunken tattered couch
and drank the sun tea she offered.

She said,
I am so sorry I have not called you back.
I have been afraid of what you might
have to tell me about my son.

I know he is struggling at school.
He comes home crying.

Our family has been through so much
these last few years.

My son has had to bury his grief
so he can take care of his brothers and sisters.

I work too much, and my heart is frail
since I lost a child and my husband
in the same cruel moment.

I have seen my depression become my son's.
I am so scared and so lost,
and feel I have let us all down.

Last week, he came to me in my bedroom.
I knew he heard me sobbing,
the lights were low.

He said,
Mom, don't cry, we're going to make it through.

I'm sorry I have disappointed you at school,
it's just so hard right now.

None of the students like me.
I don't like myself.

The worst part is, I can feel every single one
of my teachers not liking me, too.

If just one of them looked at me differently,
I believe I would have air to breathe
when I go there.

If I could breathe there,
I believe I could grieve there,
and let all my pain go.

Instead, I hold it all day long.
It's hard to learn like that.

•

I, this boy's teacher, was silent
as I heard his naked words
through his mother's shamed mouth.

In that moment, on that couch,
I realized that I could have been
that one teacher to pierce his obstruction
and let in his breath.

I could have stopped his suffocation,
if only I had not concluded him
in such horrible ways.

From then on, I would choose to see him
more beautifully.

That was the day I learned
a lesson I've carried all the way
up to this night:

Our conclusions touch lives,
and our touch is permanent.

JASMINE TEA

I switched from morning coffee
to jasmine tea

My students,
lives enflamed,
needed a calmer me.

On the patio at morning,
I listed in my mind
all the reasons I do this work with children.

In moments of classroom entropy,
I retrieved that list mentally,
stapled my heart to it emotionally,
recited it as prayer spiritually.

At each day's end, I found
at least one more thing to add to the list.

It served as my evening meditation,
my nighttime dream.

In the morning of next school day
I wrote it across the tablet
of my identity all over again,

a walking, breathing list
of reasons why I do this thing:

Because *you* don't,
I do this thing.

Because *you* won't,
I will this thing.

I choose to sing.
I serve to bring
their better nature into being...

The list went on in endless verses.
The greatest change occurred in *me*.

My persona took on the soothing
calm of jasmine tea.

Now, *I* was the soft soaked leaves,
while before I was self-defeating rigidity.

I had tried to get them to build model houses
with construction paper and markers
because it was *my idea*.

They wanted to build their world
with paper clips, rubber bands,
staples, popsicle sticks, and glue.

Now, I was able to let them.

They built something that grasped,
stretched, bonded, bent, gripped,
clamped, shone, leaned, folded, stood.

They built a shrine to possibility.

And I,
I kept sipping my jasmine tea.

BUFFALO

They emerge onto the track for gym class
traveling in tight groupings,
like buffalo.

Even as they giggle, tease, taunt,
scream, flirt, fight,

I know they are unsure, uncertain,
yearning, searching.

Each clumsy dare of selfhood
is followed by shy subtle glance
around parading herd for approval.

Daily, without exception,
they gain their measure of self and others.

My own unsure glances,
daring expressions of being,
can crush their tenuous hold
on this idea of who they are.

Some days, even ants are larger
than how these calves see themselves.

Then day turns over to the next.
They become inflated mountain,
unpassable forest.

Their thoughts so lost
deep in the stand of their complexity,
I can only guess what gathers by the fire
at the center of their woods.

As they become us,
trust is too much to bear.
They need convince themselves
they are *any* thing *but* us.
How else their dignity?

The games they play with each other,
those between boys and girls,
are not only games they practice.
This is how they will treat each
other as men and women.

For now though, they play games.
I stand in the middle,
blow the whistle,
announce the rules.

When I dare to pass on to them
what I have learned about how
games turn into habit seeds
for joy and pain,

when I dare to go there,
even I have no idea how
I might have just changed
the games we play.

For now,
they scream at me, demanding
that I call them beautiful

That I bow down and polish their brilliance.
This the proof to them that I can see it.

Their defiance protests to me:
I am the one and only.
I am something not seen before,
and I will not be grouped.

Yet they are younger than the young trees,
tender as April's leaves.

They move down the halls,
out onto the yard,
joined at the elbow
in sheer trepidation.

They are loud, mute, strong, vulnerable,
powerful just enough to scare me,
yet their heads hang down timidly.

They are early expressions
on a face of Earth so much older.

This world is their prairie.
They move as buffalo.

We, their bur or haven,
terminal blaze across the grass,
or watering hole of their dreams.

DEEP IN THE GARDEN

She is a farmer's daughter,
and cannot help but relate her work to the land.

At the town hall meeting, she takes a stand:

This garden is not so easy.
The carrots resist my pull.

I tear my palms and fingers,
yanking on green that shows
above dilapidated crust of soil

I am hoping root has gone to orange.

I hope that when the thing I seek
gives up being buried,
explodes from ground,
the force will not send me tumbling.

Though it would be a blessed falling.

This garden is not so easy.

How hard are we willing to work to pull
certain children from ungiving ground?

Is it true that every child is worth the same?

Not in this world.
But a place exists that counts worth differently.

That place is where I pitch my tent,
drive my stakes with a sturdy foot.

Place me in the schoolhouse,
in the courtyard,
on the dust named road.

Let my vessel there surrender
that which I cannot suppose.

That sweeping arc of miracle
the long douse souls require.

Call my message what you will.
Place my lamp where you wish.

The hungry will find their crumbs.
The thirsty will have their drink.

Need will meet its truest Love
in the fountain of my audacity.

In the end, I die of worldly values,
find my blessings in shy and tepid creek.

Some go looking for bright coins
and stones in the water.

I troll for camouflaged things
unseen against a dirty bottom,

poured over and unmoving beneath
the dominant flow.

I pull these things
out into evaporating air, where,

striations and character in my palms
there begin to show.

I blow
to further dry them off,
my heart then a sufficient buffing cloth.

I set them down on the old oak table,

stand back a step or two.

What once was blended into dirty bottom,
now reveals its mystery true.

These things are sedimentary stories,
accumulated places of finest
silt and shredded fabric.

These things are the cracked marble ball
a child treasures.

These things a board with splinters,
a leaky hull,
moldy corner,
moss at the foot of tree.

These things, the rain before we wake,
leaving a wet grass
whose watering we did not see.

These things, the fruit within
the blossom, within the bud,
within the branch, within the tree,
within the sprout, within the seed,
within the soil, within the earth,
within the world, within Creation.

This is how we see.

All that is great is born of small.
All that is modest is the consequence
of what stands tall.

This garden is not so easy.
Knees burn and stain of rocks and dirt
as we kneel, shift, lean,
plant, turn, toil.

This child began as a dream
in the girl who became a woman,
then a mother, to this child.

That child started as a song
in the boy who became a man,
then a father, to that child.

Brittleness of spirit comes after
what comes before.

First, is the encounter with
what should not be.

The child who encounters,
is the tool for change.

We have inserted her into
what should not be.

Now we must turn her,
use her as a key.

Her wound, suffering, learning, healing,
becoming, opens the door
onto the patio of what *should be*.

We, through a child's encounter,
step out into sunlight,

brown at the skin beneath the radiance
of our human possibility.

A NEW VISION

Truth is,
my mind is lashed to the idea that he
simply will not become something beautiful.

At night, I gnaw at the hefty rope
binding me to these disbeliefs.

I pray that by morning
I will have chewed my way through.

Morning comes too soon.
Too many fibers remain intact.

When I put on my clothes
for work, I keep trying
to strip off the pessimistic cloak
that makes me a ghoul before him.

He who is so young and not completed.

He who washes his hair
in the dirty water
my mind's basin provides him.

That water stains his scalp,
penetrates his pores,
becomes him.

No wonder he only smiles
when he is being trashed by peers.
Their scathing confirms his impotence.

Strangely, we sometimes prefer
to be proven right about
painful self-ideas,

rather than to be proven wrong by artists
who paint our light.

No wonder he cannot stand
to be in front of mirrors.

He is looking not be seen.

As long as he believes he is monstrous,
he will either seek to kill the monster,
or he will do what monsters do.

Truth is, I failed him
before I ever met him,
when I let acrid wishes
from jilted grown folks
join my bones.

Now, I stand in the rain
hoping something born of sky
will wash me out
and leech my bones
of their sour saturation.

Now, I open my briefcase,
search for a tonic I can drink
to give me drunken goggles.

The kind that make what is unattractive
appear to be worth taking home.

Now, I fumble in my purse
for a magic lipstick that will
force my mouth to smile at him.

My purse is fat and overburdened.
Any magic lipstick is surely
at the bottom of my mess.

Truth is, I used to be able
to Love him,

before I came to this
place that mocks my elders,
who needed no such goggles
to fall in Love.

This place where flowers
go unfertilized,
their tender waiting places
long unvisited by the
buzzing swarm of us who sentiment:

Where are the better flowers?
The ones worth touching
with my belief?

Truth is, I am sick of my many
mental lashings.
They actually make me sick.

To spend my life in a valley
where my own thoughts fill
the skies with falling things,

this is not the place
I wish to be.

I want to lead the rebellion,
drink from the courage cup
Mary McLeod Bethune
pressed to her lips.

I have the power to resurrect
my affection, to let my enchantments
burrow deep.

Today, I will chew through
the final fibers,
let what sleeps come through.

Perhaps in dormancy
it will have dreamt a reason
for me to tilt my cup
into this child's heart

and pour.

BURNING STIGMA STICKS

Some people like to pet him,
as though he is a subservient beast on four legs.

Others keep their distance.
They are the eager scavengers swiping every
artifact from the ground of his world,
as though each broken shard
is evidence of his inferiority.

They take their trinkets
to the lab of their presumption,
where they run lazy tests
on faulty machines spitting flawed algorithms,

ultimately pronouncing this child's
being as carrier of a bubonic plague
or some such reason to quarantine
him behind glass walls
of indifference or scorn or both.

Others eschew this dark archaeology,
reasoning that if only the dust were
rinsed off the pieces,
their idea of the artist would grow in esteem.

These traitors to the caste system
sit close to the child,
run their fingers through
his smooth ambrosia.

This stroke releases his long encumbered
amber incense.

Precious collections, left behind
by his hopeful ancestors
inside the far corners of his
fundamental chambers,
commence to remember
they still have use.

Especially in this young and dying culture,
these fine endowments shift and hum.

Once ruptured child becomes a chalice,
his mind, once barren shack,
is now a palace,
its walls ornate with masterpieces.

Child ablaze now surrenders his outer walls,
moats, and guards,

lowers his ladders,
extends his bridges.

Forest of the world around him
incinerates before his purpose born.

What grows up after
through ash and haze
is a stand of believing trees.

All because adults like you and these
sat close to him and ran your fingers
through his smooth ambrosia.

CALLING ALL RIVERS

His inspiration comes from something
his great uncle said to him from a bowlegged
rocking chair on a weathered porch in August:

We have too many dams,
not nearly enough rivers.

It takes a broken heart
to unleash compassion's holy flow.

We have too many dams and walls,
too much hardness, toughness,
callousness, smugness, arrogance.

These separation walls keep us from Love:
Our own Love.
The Love of others.

Our world dies for lack of irrigation.

A mighty generational river surges,
bangs against our tall barricades
trying to break through.

We have spliced it in contradiction,
made it to snake down crazy canyons,
narrow and shallow in the flats.

No vital flow can follow our ill laid maze.

We sit heavy and unyielding
on what we believe to be thrones of knowing.

Instead, we are stuffing Brilliance back down
into its disbelieving burrows.

We reign over hollow kingdoms.
Nobody lives in the chateaus we pillory
with fantasies of domination and control.

A small thing takes its drink
from the well in the courtyard,
nervous and skittish that we will lance it from
the blind side for violating our code of ethics,

a law that speaks of prohibition against
creative displays and the exercising of quirks
and talents not writ in the
Great Black Book of Normalcy.

A small thing takes its drink,
waits for the shadows to descend.

Who will be its protector?
Whose heart will break enough
to be flooded with Love?

VILLAGE HEALER

How much breaking should
I allow my heart today?

Which stories should I hold onto in a way
that leaves them bleeding all over me?

Which ones should I wash away?

How human should I be
in the midst of this inhumanness?

They want me to make progress
in this teeming mine field,

even as they harness my mine detector
with dictates of polluted politics.

This child is given one oar
and expected to steer straight
on the boundless river.

That one never sleeps.
This one cannot stop sleeping.

Both are on the run from monsters
we have made.

This one mourns her drinking father
as he plods on toward his grave.

This one thinks she has to be
a woman for her siblings,
peddles her body as we have taught.

It occurs to me that I need to learn
something more about Love
and how to deliver affection,

for teaching rests on the ability to transmit
to a child *that you care.*

I endeavor to become the village healer,
who with mortar and pestle,
grinds grandmother's herbs
into a potent salve to cure:

This one's running nose.
This one's busted upper lip.
This one's stinking clothes.
This one's front tooth chip.

And to treat the blindness of the royal court,
who fail to recognize:

This one's regal posture.
This one's royal ways.

This one's dimpled smile.
This one's downcast glance.

And in each, a shy romance.

Yes, I take on the cloak of the sturdy ancestors,
who simply chose, as a matter of fact,
to let their hearts break

all the way.

TRUTH ENCRUSTED THRONE

The new worker is charged by her supervisor
with creating her own professional pledge.

She sits by a river and meditates.
Society leaves her thoughts,
insight takes its place.

She writes,

My mantras:

Smile at him, for he may
receive none at home.

Respect him, because I may be
his solitary oasis of esteem.

Forgive him, because his landscape
is littered with bear traps
ready to punish him to the bone
for every slight misstep.

Expect of him, for his days
are a dark eclipse of non-expectation.
Let my faith in him be his light.

Let my persistent effort
be a tourniquet for his hemorrhaging
temptation to give up.

Teach him.
In too many moments he is not being taught.

Translate his tongue.
He speaks in low avoidant code
to conceal that he is afraid and unknowing.

See beyond his mask.

His hard outer shell protects
a tender flesh of heart.

His apparent disinterest is his response
to a world that has been disinterested
in him.

Learn his story.
It is my path to understanding his way
of existence.

Withhold judgment.
He is the manifestation of every
judgment passed against him.

Share my story.
It may be his first glimpse
of my humanness.

Provide him a room for laughter
in the home of our relationship.

Counteract every assault
on his dignity by taking a stand
that risks social disapproval.
Be his Amazing Grace.

Thank him silently for giving me
the opportunity to practice patience.

Do not ever stop excavating
until I reach the layer of his beauty.
His sediment can wash me clean
if I learn how to sift it through my own.

Remember, he is a social myth.

Daily, in my mind, build for him
a truth encrusted throne.

VINES TO TRESTLE

A cold wind blows
through the heart of those
who believe themselves free
in such a way they need not participate
in humanity.

The cold therein steels the heart to harden.
Weeds grow where should be a garden.

Pardon never may come to those who run
from this final intimacy,
this dissolving in the human sea.

Greedy be we who clutch ourselves closed
on crutch of homogeneity and similarity,
based on fear and insecurity.

The hurt we do is to ourselves and our kin,
more so than to the quilt, human and free.

For who but Madness believes it may
separate its grain of dust from desert wide,
its slice of water from ocean's bath.

What soul shouts "I am!",
but is not truly being, human,
which is to say:

We on this earth breathe not air
but one another.
In isolation souls do smother.

Would we but dare to open up,
joy's breath would fill our spirit cup.

This social world is our drinking water.
What fool pollutes her drink with prejudice,
when she can purify it with tonic of her heart.

Relationship is our holy vessel,
binding fast our vines to trestle.

Those vines be our generations
seeking bloom.
Our compassion heeds them room.

Our own children feel the stroke
of tender human spoke
on Creation's turning wheel,

and bear us gifts by their becoming,
not fractured souls but music humming.

One day, the song, full and flush,
but first Compassion, its seeds in us,
to lay in music's underbrush.

I RESIST

I have been taught an idea of him
that is a sin.

It starts in his skin,
snakes through his tongue,
tinges the air with the song he has sung.

And yet, I was born with a heart
better than this,
so I resist.

I resist the talcum blanching of prejudice.
My *own people* have taught this
idea of him.

And though I Love them, my own people,
I will not betray his youthful right
to wear his skin and be treated

to the absence of my prejudice.

So, I resist.

My colleagues clown his manner
of speech, even as their whispered
viper hiss is an awful lisp.

And though I would bypass social
friction if I were to join them in this,

I will not let beat a single sounding
of my heart's malice
at his speaking of his native tongue.

Though generations spread
the weary myth of his subhumanness,
I will not do this.

I am pressed to judge him
in the context of his otherness.

I will not.
His beauty springs from the source
of Providence.

And though most are blind to the
genius of his expression,

I will not hang his good works
in the closet of my shamefulness.

His will go on my central walls of gallery.
His notions will join my jubilee.

And if a monarch butterfly should slide
down breeze to rest on me,
I shall see him in that precious monarchy.

As others sweep him into their noxious
mental cyst,
I will lean him into a gentler mist.

Oh, we callous calcified heart stained masses,
we know not what we do.

He is a notion brighter than all of this.
His dying is our own in time.

His glory slakes the world of thirst.

I have pitched my splintered stake
in his unsung ground.

And, come the noise of lies to break him down,
come this unspeakable mourning sound,

I will resist.

I AM A TEACHER

He shares his dream with the group
near the conclusion of the retreat:

In my dream, a child spoke:

"When you beheld me as a baby, as a newborn
soul, my skin did not frighten you, nor did my
voice, though as yet unskilled. Now as I stand
before you, a child still, though larger, with voice
more pronounced—now I am to you not
something to be cradled and sung to, but a
deviation from your comfort zone, to be
controlled and scorned. I am only a child, and
even though I may act out, I do so only as you do
so, because I am uncertain of my role. Who am
I—my teacher—that your adoration for me has
grown so cold?"

The man continues:

Those words captured me in a dream last night, and I was ransomed by the fright. For my freedom, I surrendered blindness, and now I must ask myself this: What wicked wind has, as the child said, blown me so cold? Are not these children here, the ones I now fear, the same children whose infant preciousness gave me desire to swoop them up, diapers and all, and cuddle and cradle and kiss them without end?

This is what I believe:

I am a teacher, potent and proud. I am a teacher, a preacher, a listening ear. I'll not forget who I am, regardless the weather, regardless the tempest that churns in this dizzying world.

I am a teacher, potent and proud. And I must know that mine is not the task of imparting knowledge, but that of letting it bloom. Nor should I tarry too long on bending the young to kneel at my power. My true power, my given gift, is that of lifting up, not forcing a kneeling rift.

The daily frustrations at the hands of these young, I can recount easily in my sleep—the fighting, the disrespect, the absence, and lack of effort; the enduring sway of their emotional pain. But if I look closely I can see that their frustrations are truly mine, for their behaviors are only the outpouring of genuinely human needs.

In their search for identity, I see my own striving for a role amongst an increasingly unfamiliar student crowd. In their search for belonging, I, too, am reflected, for if I feel so at home, then why do I fight so hard to claim my turf? They are disillusioned, disheartened, and of low self-esteem. Their emotions are bottled up; they have no place to scream. But if these aren't also forces welled up in my own chest, then all my life has been but a dream.

Feeling inadequate to the task of rightly handling these Every Persons, and their cultural needs, my security is not adult-like; it is juvenile, it bleeds. How am I to be the gender, ethnic, linguistic, religious, and cultural caretaker? These issues I have not even fully satisfied within myself, and so I seek shelter in what I teach. But what DO I teach?

We are teachers, potent and proud, but we must know our place, we must not crowd. We are the *fertilizer*, but not the *fertility*. The fertility is theirs because they are the Young. It is now their turn and this is their stage.

This, too, I believe:

I am the Black child's brother and sister. The Latino are *mi raza*, my race. I AM of the Asian persuasion. I am Russian, and an American Indian, and I... am all over the place.

The wheelchair-bound student over there near the stage... I must push, not against her chair, but against her spirit, to climb, to leap, to dare.

The young boy who speaks a language I cannot make out, I must understand that, far from being a threat, he is a whole new world to explore; here before me, without travel, a brand new shore.

I am all people at once, for to be culturally any of these, one need only be human first. The second need is simply to spend some time in a culture's midst. In this I am well qualified, because each culture that walks through my classroom doors, I breathe in as if it were air. Therefore, in essence, my hair is both straight and kinky, my skin both dark and fair.

To encounter such varied and wondrous new life, courageous curiosity has often in the history of our world had to sail and traverse, and climb, and battle, and freeze and starve. But here sit I, at the head of a frenzied court, while an endless stream of discovery places itself in my rooms, in my halls, in my hands.

This unsettling time, burgeoning with unforeseen possibilities and visions, is not the time to wither away in fear. Nor is it the time to bellow an intimidating stand of power to allay the insecurities we find so hard to accept. We are teachers—sunshine sent to glare upon a vastly flowing garden. How dare we burn too brightly and make limp our tender youth? How dare we shroud them in the cold of our frightened stooping behind clouds of habit? We are the Sun... how could we so coldly dare?

As a teacher I also know this:

I am a teacher, and whether I ply my craft in the classroom or the lunchroom; whether with a globe or a lathe; with a beaker, a bandage, or a conductor's wand; whether I drive the bus, or counsel the troubled, or maintain the buildings, or monitor the halls, I am an adult in a land of children, and their eyes are upon me. I am teaching even when I know not that I am.

I must be thoughtful, quick-minded, curious, and pensive, as they are. I must be responsive, flexible, and ever-surprising, as they, too, are. I must learn, as they do. I must absorb and grow; and give some to get some, as I expect of them. To the extent that I demand their ear, I must also lend mine, for a child's worst fear is of the self's voice gone unheard. So I must gather their every word, and treat it as gold. I must make harvest of their words, in bushels of opportunity for growth. In doing so, I must show them how to make harvest of their own words, so they may become producers of the products we all consume in this world: creativity, skills, talents, insight, and achievements out of sight.

I must treat them each as dignitaries from their own unique foreign lands. The red carpet I roll out should be strewn with confirmation, expectation, and appreciation. My dignitary gifts should be wrapped in the provision that I will do all that I can to bring the world I know to them in a way that allows them to bring their world to me, and to their child peers.

I will serve as a scaffold, a bridge, between what has been, for better or for worse, and what they will bring into being, also for better or for worse. They have as much right as all others who have trounced and tripped on this Earth to make their own footprints. If they be footprints of gold, or footprints unworthy, they will be THEIR footprints, for I will not have held them hostage in the sky, bound by my arms, left with feet dangling in despair. I will make them care.

I also know that if I do not give shelter with equal kindness to all of the children in these halls, I will have endangered myself; for when a child is harmed, with no remedy on hand, only negativity will sprout from the wound. So I must give voice to the voiceless, and I must have the security not to shrink from the unfamiliar languages, customs, and attitudes in my presence.

I am a teacher, potent and proud, and I *will* have the strength to recognize that the very forces I fear, these children fear, too. Their troubles and struggles are born of that brew. If I expect that they come correct to my table, then I must ask: How have I cleansed my own hands? I am bound to shed hypocrisy by scrubbing more heartedly at the dirt I carry: my harmful views, fostered by my own unheard, unexplored childhood truths.

If not for the world that my children, and their children will occupy, then FOR myself I must no longer TO myself lie. I am a teacher, and so I must teach, I must reach... the hearts of these students here. Soon they will either ascend to positive adulthood, pulling me up alongside, or they will descend into adulthood's dungeon of despair, and pull me down, too, for they will have no care.

I must cleanse from my heart the negative pulses. I know they can sense my true pulse like a strong scent on my skin. So I will do this thing—I will teach, I will preach, I will reach their hearts and make them stand tall in their childhood land. I will face honestly my faults, and not beat myself down. Like them, I am a child in the sense of my tenure in this new world of theirs; and I will misstep, but at least I will have stepped at all.

I will do this because I am a teacher, potent and proud, and mine is the doorway through which I must let *all* children pass. My potency will uplift them, and as they triumph, so shall I. As they find their place in the world, so shall I know mine. I will teach because I am a teacher, and I must.

I *must* teach.

AFTER SCHOOL

At the head of the path
 that leads through the woods,
slender boy runs up to the playground monitor,
his voice too worn for his age:

Will you walk me home?

Sure, son.
So, did you have fun in school today?

My uncle beats me.
My auntie plays with my no-no places.

Paralyzed for a moment by the sheer
overwhelming scope of this truth,
the man stops, searches for words.

Not knowing what else to do,
he places a gentle hand on the boy's shoulder.
They walk to the ice cream parlor
and talk baseball and girls.

It is all he can offer in that moment.

It is more than has been offered
to a slender boy all day.

Hurt is paved over in a fine dusting of reprieve.
The moment, though fleeting, is priceless,
a reservoir of joy to be dearly recalled
in the long moments to follow.

A HOME FOR YOU

It is a conference for adults
who advocate for disconnected youth.

The opening speaker
begins to recite a recipe
for what youth need, saying:

Our children need a place to call home—

Just then, a youth in the audience
rises and says:

Excuse me, but I've been thinking...

In the garden,
by the brook,
a thought came to me,
and once settled, took.

You who work on my behalf
also need a place to call home.

You need a running stream
in the form of lasting connections
to those with whom you toil.

You need Loving families,
circles of associates
in the office and on the road.

You need colleagues who care
for you and dare to lift your load.

The price you pay for this mission
is steep indeed.

You need supportive peers
to polish your tarnished shine,
especially in the winter of a nation
whose warmth has withered on the vine.

You, too, need a safe place to live,
for while you work and give,
your spirit is a tender thing
that needs and hurts and *is*.

Someone needs to help you learn
to take good care of yourself.

We youth cannot afford
for your wellness to lose its light.
We need your strongest flame on our behalf,
your brightest glow for this precious fight.

The way you do this work
should not leave your soul impoverished.

Your days should be built on bricks
of relationship that bring assets to your life.

All the ideas you generate to usher us
toward our golden potential gate
should shine on us in such a way
that they reflect off us
and shine on you,
deepening the cup of *your* dignity.

Where has frivolity fled?
I cannot find it in your eyes,
you've lost the happiness
you meant to share with
the very youth that now
walk eclipsed in your shadowed song.

You've not done wrong,
you've just lost your way.
Your compass of identity
is rusted and nearly broke.

Remember, you came into this
because you dared to dream
of a greater bliss for those like me.

it is time to stop and drink
from a cleaner water,
refresh your inner spring.

There is such a thing
as suffering the cruel offspring
of a nation's negligence,

and fighting with due diligence
for justice for our youth,
while still managing to grasp and cling
to the very thing that lets you sing:

The soul inside,
the softer hide,
the fertility for your merriment.

Never ask where happy went,
it never goes away.

It just grows discouraged
when our heart, open,
is pierced and then,
our joy leaks out.
Hope loses hold,
and fears of old
rise up to block the light.

Never ask where happy went.
Joy is a seed that grows in the soil sold
to a life devoted to humanity.

Joy once was a sunflower standing tall.
Watered faithfully, joy can live again.

A child is not the only one
who needs the caress
of a Loving summer sun.
You who toil need this, too,
a social family of caring folks
where celebrated spirits roam.

In the garden,
by the brook,
a thought came to me
and once settled, took.

Adults also need a place to call home.

HARVESTING HOPE

An elder woman sat me down to talk.
She noticed the fatigue pulling at my face.

She said, No, no...
Don't you give up on me now.
Don't you go to sleep on me,
on them.
You're almost there.
You've come too far.

Her skin was beautifully wrinkled,
portraying the terrain of her life.

Her hair, wonderfully grayed
so it could reflect the sunlight
and share that illumination with others.

Her eyes, magnificently clouded with cataract,
so she could see with a higher vision.

She said,
Youngblood,
I have seen a better day on down
this dust caked road.
I might not get there with you,
but I know a way.

She said,
When the children are scattered,
gather them up.

When families are in jeopardy,
lift them up.

When communities are in disarray,
find the courage,
take matters into your own hands,
mend the fabric.

When the sky grows dark,
seek not shelter from beyond yourself,
but seek it from *within* yourself.

I asked her,
Dear Ma'am,
how do we accomplish this?

She said,
Very simply.
You all got to accumulate your wisdom.

Wisdom.
That sweet nectar of life
that drips down the vines of generation,
and percolates through the pores
of mothers and fathers,
and comes to rest upon our lips,
where, if only we open ourselves,
we may taste of it,

and become whole again.

FIREFLIES

I, being a teacher,
forewent the temptation to judge,

instead, huddled myself behind the visage
of spirits dancing,

caught the brilliance
of their surges and rhythms,
and, like a visitor from a distant place,
beheld this obvious expression of a Great artist.

Then, breathing more deeply,
eyes blinking to confirm my sight,
form began to coalesce around these spirits.

I beheld them as children,
early-life beings I knew well from my days.

But these,
I saw in new light,
with Creation Itself emanating from the very
breast of theirs.

I realized their dance was rightful to them,
as were their smiles,

so, too, the wisps of translucent color drifting
tendrils from their bodies.

I knew these silken wanderings as dream states,
for they carried concentrations of a most
intensified light:

Ebbing balls of imagery and affection,
they found their way to the ceiling,
there, clouding over us as confection.

In this moment, I was thankful
of my initial hesitation to judge,

to judge the frantic darting about,
the chattering, buzz, piercing screams,
belly laughter, pushing, pulling,

tugging, leap-frogging,
piggy-backing, karate-chopping,

crying, pouting, name-calling,
hand-holding, why-the-sky-is-blue?
we missed you...

For here were bulbs of midday brightness,
cloaked in gangly forms,
costumed in cloth of hope-to-be,
scattering in their movement toward sky.

Never again would I witness this dance
and see not first
their spirit core fluttering about,

fireflies dominating their outer forms,
weaving wisps of imagery in dreams above
to sweetly dust the day.

MUTUALITY

On twin swings
they breeze back and forth, side by side,
woman and girl.

The younger says, in a canary's voice,
Close your eyes... okay... now...

Do you see me?
If so, you seed me. I take root in you.

Do you feel me?
If so, you feed me.
I fill my well with water clean.

Do you hear me?
If so, you heal me.

Understanding is the medicine I need.

Will you be my *student*?
If so, I will teach,
and in teaching, I will learn from you.

In marriage, two make a sacred pledge as one.

In this relationship we cannot be one
without a pledge from two:

that you will seek my magnificence,
and I will seek yours, too.

MS. TINA

She
skips rope to the beat
of chocolate milk surging
down a parched
12-year-old throat
in high July.

Her
bare feet bouncing for relief
off the street,
heart beat moving fleet,
dreams dancing in her head
of when her family will
be whole again...
because she feels:

If
we can just get it
together we'll be okay,
cause we are family,
can't nobody take that away from us,
can they?

That night
in the glow of street light,
hidden under the sheets,
she takes pencil to paper,
feeds her journal these words:

My greatest fears:

She writes,

and as she writes, the words
are also written on the blackboard
inside her mind,
etched on the inner walls
of her heart,
where they will stay,
stubborn graffiti
hidden in the shadows
but persistent all the same.

And she writes

My greatest fears:

Mommy dying,
Daddy crying,
bad things under the bed,
somebody taking my family away,
away.

I know a way
to keep bad things away,
I'll pray...

I'll do like Ms. Johnson
at the library
when people come at her mean,
I'll look at them scary,
I'll build a wall around my heart,
that way no fires can start
inside my chest
that would escape from
there and burn the rest of me.

I'm afraid, cause people

don't seem to like my family.
They don't say so with their mouths,
they speak it with their looks.

Wish I had me some cookbooks
for all the crooks who
come to steal our joy.
I'd make me up a meal
so hot and spicy,
they would have to ask *us* for water.
Least for once they'd be asking *us* for something.
Seems like we're always asking
somebody else for something,

then they always give us that look,
like we are something less,
and they are something more,
but they don't know my godmother,
she can sing like an angel.
They don't know my
best friend Keisha,
can't nobody add
numbers as fast as she can.

They don't know my Uncle Roy,
I've seen him make a gourmet meal
from nothin' but flour and water,
seem like to me.

My Daddy, he may not be fancy
but he can dance with Mommy
real sweet and make her feel like
somethin' special when he dips her down.

And Mommy, she may not have
all the best dresses and shoes,
and she may not talk smart-like,
but she knows more ways to
stretch a dollar than those folks
in suits and nice cars always
stressin' they budget and fussin'
'bout they stocks and *bombs*.

And my family,
we sure can tell some stories,
keep you laughin' most the night.
Stories 'bout folk we know
and some we don't,
don't wanta know either,
and stories 'bout Moses
and Ms. Harriet Tubman
and Jesse Owens,
stories that make you feel
good about yourself.
Yeah we can light a fire
with stories and keep
the house warm 'til
morning light.

I just hope nobody ever takes
me away,
cause how would I ever find
my way back,
and why are people always talking
about sending me to a better life.
Folk seem awful comfortable
with the idea of me never seeing
my family again.

I read my books,
I remember they used to do that
to slave children,
send them away to a better life.
I bet in the Master's house
when trouble came,
the children didn't get sent
to a better life.
Seem like folk think children like me
weren't ever supposed to be with
our own families in the first place.

Yessum,
I read my books...
They took certain other children away, too,
they called it making them civilized.
They used to cut off all their hair.
Us, they take us and cut off our memories.

But what if I don't want no better life?
What if I just want *my* Mommy
and to play with *my* brother
and keep going to *my* school
and never ever split up with *my* friends?

So what Mommy's not doing well,
I'll go stay with Big Ma,
she Loves me, too,
and if not Big Ma,
more than two people in my family Love me,
ain't that true?

I get so tired I just want to sleep
and wake up and us have everything we need.

I don't need another family,
I just want people to stop being so mean to us.
It makes my Daddy cry.

Now, that Ms. Tina
from the agency, she for real.
I'll tell you how I know...
Most folk don't look me in the eye
when they speak to me,
I mean they do,
but really they just lookin' right past me
like I'm a ghost or something
and they just talkin' to the wind.

Ms. Tina, she looks me in the eye.
I can feel her gaze settle on my soul,
and when I speak or even when I don't
I can *feel her* listening to me...
Now that's some real stuff.

Yeah, Ms. Tina,
she's not like some other folk,
I've even seen her look at Mommy
like Mommy's a real person...
Ms. Tina don't know,
but after she leaves,
Mommy floats around the house
like a queen or something.
I like that cause I don't
think most people see Mommy's beauty.
Does being poor make your beauty
invisible?

Ms. Tina, she talks to Daddy
like he's a full grown Man,

not a boy...
Seem like if you're a man like Daddy
in this world,
if you stand up all the way they beat you down,
and if you crouch down,
they smile and pat your back.
Daddy wasn't made for that I don't think,
but after Ms. Tina leaves I notice Daddy
treats Mommy better,
heck,
he treats us all better.

Ms. Tina, she don't know that.

It must be hard for Ms. Tina
working with all these families like ours,
cause it seems she don't have much support.

Some days I see her dragging her spirit around
behind her like it's about to fall off in the dirt
and get lost.

I wonder if a spirit is like an umbilical cord,
wonder if you cut it loose does it shrivel
up and die.

Hope I never see that happen with Ms. Tina,
cause then who would treat us right?

And who's gonna believe in us?
I think it must hurt a soul a whole heap
to have the whole world not believe in 'em
except for one person.

Wonder if that's what Jesus felt like
when they strung him up on the cross...
Poor Jesus,
he didn't have no Ms. Tina by his side.

Sometimes I feel like everybody wants to
crucify our family for being the way we are,
like we did something wrong by not having
money and making mistakes...
Don't the people who get to keep their children
make mistakes, too?
Who's there to scold them?

I remember the time Ms. Tina thought
Ricky and me might have to get put
with another family,
or at least in another home.
I remember how she sat with us
and made us call all the relatives together
to talk and figure out what to do.
I remember how she kept asking
us about our strengths.
I thought she meant who had the most muscles.
Later I realized she meant how did we
deal with our troubles.

She kept pushin' at us and pushin' at us,
trying to help us help ourselves.
Eventually we found a way
for Ricky and me to stay in the family
while Mommy got better.
Auntie Ruth took us in for a while,
but at least my nightmare never came true,
they never took my family away.

But you know what?
I do believe that if ever Ms. Tina
had to put Ricky and me in another family,
I do believe she would pick a good one for us,
not any ol' family...
I trust Ms. Tina cause
I think we mean something to her...
Most people when they come in our house
they look around and start frownin'.

Ms. Tina,
she comes in and her eyes always light up
when she sees us.
I don't know if she's just fakin',
far as not likin' what she sees around the house,
cause our house, there's not much in it,
but at least she cares enough about
our feelings to fake like she's happy to see us.
At least she cares enough to act like we mean
something. That's more than we're used to.

But Ms. Tina,
I think she really does care...
If I was the people running the agency,
I'd pay her a million dollars
cause that's what she's worth.

Every time I sleep through the night
and wake up and my nightmare
hasn't come true,
that's when I think Ms. Tina
is worth more than gold.

When I grow up
I'm going to make something

with my life,
just so I can turn around
and thank my Mommy and Daddy
and Ms. Tina,
the three big people
who always made me feel like I
was the sunshine
even when the rain was making them wet.

Ms. Tina,
I know I don't appear to be friendly
on the surface,
but that's just cause I'm scared
that if I smile
that's where the pain will sneak in
and come back to visit my heart.

•

She turns the page in her journal
and writes these last words:

My greatest fears:

Mommy dying,
Daddy crying,
bad things under the bed,
somebody taking my family away.

p.s.
Ms. Tina:

Someday I'm gonna help all the
children just like you do.
You ain't just my hero,
you're my angel, too.

You take good care of yourself.
I need you to.

12-year-old closes her book,
emerges from under the sheets,
drifts off to sleep
as fireflies mimic the stars...

Nightmare chased away for
yet another night.

JOB DESCRIPTION

Her supervisor hands her a card celebrating
her one-year anniversary on the job.

Initially, the young lady had been unsettled
that her work with adjudicated youth
escaped the neatly outlined ideas of her
graduate school textbooks
and ran into the margins in bright red scrawl.

With her supervisor's patient guidance,
she had grown into the reality of textured lives.

The anniversary card reads:

The soul of social work is compassion.
Not passion, knowledge, experience,

but compassion:
the capacity and habit of wishing for others
that they do not suffer,
then acting on that wish.

This habit takes work, thus the term *social work.*
Not social games, social exercise, or social hobby.
Social work.

Casually interested folks need not apply.

All praise to the *work* in *social*
and to the souls who do the work.

PREPARING THE FLOCK

At the parent-teacher conference
she makes a promise:

I will not train them to test,
I will nurture them to grow,
for life's true tests care nothing
for multiple choice questions
or fill in the blank supposition.

If I do not teach them to learn,
and to Love learning,
to imagine, believe, forgive,
remember, receive, honor,
respect, dare, delight,
dance, sing, sorrow,
surrender to silence,

if I do not teach them *all* of this,
I lead them only to slaughter,
fattened on synthesized pastures
of standardized testing grain.

Life's challenges care nothing for standards.
They come at us in waves that mock
the tests for which we prepare our children.

CHERRY BLOSSOMS

My heart speaks now to you,
the one who would serve to toil
on my behalf.

I am the child of your daily labor,
of your nightly dreams.
Let me show you something.

But wait, I must warn you:

What is to be seen lies this way,
far within my private garden
in the depths of my treasure chest.

Come unto me, but come unto me true.
To venture here you must walk naked
and crying, for no cloth must mask your
own frailty.

Tears must cleanse you well,
lest you infect my soul,
the very thing you
dare invite yourself beside.

I have stories for you,
they begin like this:

You see me as small and weak,
yet my spirit is the ocean.
My tide has crept along your shore.

I have witnessed your secrets,
you bear them alone and shivering.

Your garden has gone cold,
but now is the season in which
you will choose to die or to live.

Know that this choice is my fate, too:
As you die or live, I die or live with you.

Our spirits are bound as such.
At night, you cry out to God:
Why have you done this to this poor child?

You do not hear God's response:
*What I have done to this poor child, I, too,
have done to you.*

My own cry is different in those same nights.
I cry: *God why have you done this
to the grown ones who toil for me, the child,
that they cannot see my Truth?*

So, you see, we are two souls,

each crying for the other,
forming rivers of tears that
go ungathered.

Your garden has gone cold,
the chill wilts my youthful flower.

You cry for me, yet your own struggle
steals my sunlight.

It is time for you to release your cherry
blossoms and cloud the sky.

What then rains down will cleanse your
vision and you will see me true.

You will see that as you question
why you do this work,
my child heart questions
why you began this work,

whose life you serve in bearing this work,
when will you at last betray this work
and therefore betray me.

You will see that though you have
seen me as poor and pitiable,
I am rich and blessed.

You see my family roots as rotten,
but fail to see that we are a worthy
tree that feeds on rotten ground.

Your heart Loves me, but your mind
judges me.

You see my chocolate skin as
evidence that I come from something
burnt and broken,

so you dream for me of places
bright and distant.

My roots are not burnt or barren,
only brushed and blemished,
yet firm and fertile,
my family still has beauty left to forge.

You despair about my well fare,
I wonder when you will say fare well

Stress is a storm sweeping
your valley into dusk,
my future in your hands
is your own sunrise.

What you touch in me in winter
becomes my gift to you in June.

You fear you make no change in
my life,
but you forget the darkness
you keep from my life.

You suffer a starving pocket,
are paid light of coin for your work,
yet are made rich every moment
of this mission.
You look for your payment
in the wrong purse.

You spin webs of gold on the fabric

of our childhood futures,
but look for fool's gold in false streams.

Your heart desires approval for the
battles you fight.
Look to your own echo for that.
We create the world in which we live.

You wonder how much you can afford
to bleed for me, but your blood
is your own salvation.

We eat the fruit of seeds we sow.
Child welfare is a harvest of faith,
its true rewards run latent, blossom later,
as I grow into the adult who raises
a family like the ones you dream for me.

So, here we are together,
you wish beauty upon me,
you *are* the beauty upon me.

You have not only come to me,
I have come to you,
your work is my ministry,
your Love is my bread,
your endurance my breath,
your desire my warmth,

your pain my hope,
your courage my strength,
your tears my drink,
your nightmares my audience,
your faith my shelter.

I am your child,
but here in my garden you are *my* child,
I give birth to your glory
every day that I live.

Now you see me, don't you?
Good, because that is why you are here,

this is why we bleed,
so that we may send our cherry blossoms
to the sky.

I KNOW YOU

You
are the ones asked to step into heartbreak
and break no hearts,
especially not your own.

You are expected to step into private lives
and gain the trust of people
for whom trust has long since departed.

You're the ones who have to
find a way to bring parenting skills
to people who see you as a stranger,
trying to teach them a class
they never signed up for,
and what's more,
feel they already have a degree in.

You're the ones who have to

make decisions that bleed
and then defend them to
those who were never there
to see the truth of these families.

You're the ones charged
with keeping a family together
when society screams out:
Take those children away from there!

You're the ones responsible
for placing children out of home
when society screams:
Keep that family together!

You're the ones expected
to keep everyone dry
regardless the weather.

It's you who is told
to go make sandcastles
out of mud puddles,
and don't drag any of
that dirt back to the office,
much less home with you at night.

It's you who has
this much time,
this much energy,
and *this many* resources
to take on *this much* pain,
this much fear,
this many families,
this many dreams,

and turn it all into a happy ending
before *this much* spirit dies and fades away.

I know you.

I saw you creeping down by the river
one night,
leaving your footprints in the mire
as you screamed at the water
and waited for the waves
to grow angry and swallow you up.

I saw the smile on your face
and the celebration in your heart
when the family you worked with
discovered that they were valid, valuable,
and held Divine light,
and the Divine right and responsibility
to come together around a child.

I saw the tension leave your body
and the relief come calling,
both in the same breath,
when you saw that the child placement
you made had grown blossoms
and was reaching for the sky.

I've seen you in your moments of doubt,
Why am I doing this,
your moments of joy,
That's why I'm doing this,
your moments of quiet pride,
this child is our future.

I know you.

You give us hope,
you give us life,
for a child is life,
and the path between chaos
and freedom
contains a point of birth.

You are that daring midwife,
that sweet vicious Harriet Tubman,
that uppity Nat Turner,
humble, proud, angry,
Loving, enduring,
never relenting,
always repenting,
emergency rescue unit
without the uniform,
paycheck,
status,
flashing lights.

All you do
is get up off the canvass
and win your fights.

Glorious,
Godly,
Goodness,
your name is Grace.

I know you.

A SPECIAL KIND

While others hypothesize, theorize, and rationalize,

Social Workers revolutionize, empathize, and dry teary eyes.

Others gesticulate and regulate.

Social Workers educate, illuminate, and elevate.

Others fantasize, mesmerize, stigmatize, criminalize, demonize.

Social Workers dispense with lies, *and still they rise.*

Some cast stones and mud.

Social Workers build the dam, hold back the fatal flood.

Some protest and donate.

Social Workers wade in the water, testify, and agitate.

Some take families and make war.

Social Workers take families and make warriors.

Others dictate, subordinate, manipulate,
placate, salivate, come too late, gyrate, orate,

speculate, procrastinate, increase the rate,
irritate, expect poor fate, feed the hate, clean
the fiscal plate, lock the gate.

Our dear children bear all this weight.

Social Workers, they just take it all in and
alleviate, alleviate, alleviate.

In the morning, when Sun rises, new Light
shines because a Social Worker is awake.

COMET SHOWER

He wants to remind himself of the need
for humility when anger or expectation
would be the easier thing.

So each morning he reads to himself
the note that he keeps on his mirror:

I am not here to change him,
but to be changed by him.

In allowing him to touch my soul,
I will have evidence of my success,
success in getting out of the way
of his Divine becoming,

by standing in the middle of his stream,
letting him witness how *he* touches *me*.

I must let him be audience to his greatness
impacting me.

He is a home-bound comet shower
pocking my surface with beauty marks.

Entering my atmosphere,
he blazes, trailing sparks,

and I, open-mouthed,
amazed as he showers the sky
with the brilliance he brings to me.

COURAGE TO TAKE THE SHOT

Though he has been the child's advocate,
he is surprised when the boy asks him:

Will you come to my game?

Sure, son, but won't your father be there?

Yes.

And your brothers and sisters?

Yes.

Your friends?

Yes.

So, I am curious why you care so much
about me being at your game.

Because, you always stand up for me,
even when it means risking your job.
Not many people take a chance on me.
I figured you must believe in me
to do something like that.

And I thought,
if you can take a chance on me,
I can take a chance on life.

I figured, if you are at my game,
I will remember your courage,
and I won't be afraid to take the shot.

RETIREMENT LETTER

Dear Administration,
with these words I pen
to you my retirement letter:

My tears tattoo the mountains
of my paperwork now abandoned
in your catacombs of files,
never again to see the light of

consideration or review,

entombed more finally than a
royal family inside audacious crypt.

My tears tattoo my paperwork,
their long trails announcing
like warrior paint across my cheekbones
my every good intent
to prevent tragedy to my village,

to beat back what aggresses
against our children,

and yet, as I walk on hard earned
calluses into vague cloud of my
what comes next,
I am deeply vexed.
My years of service have brought me
to this epiphany:

What aggresses against our dearest young
is neither external nor unannounced.

Indeed, it lives within.

Our laws are serpentine,
their consequence snakes avoidant path
around our young,

a drunken delta of tributaries
that deliver any goodness they might hold
to the ocean of adult cares.

They finger from lofty plateaus

of lobbyist lips, down the slopes of policy,

landsliding over saplings
with rippling brutal force,
unbridled on their course
to making someone *grown* content,

perhaps paying handsomely those
who see the angle.

Our young all around them, seeking water,
little of it reaching them at the root.

Too much deviation for law
to reach its good intent.

Too many pockets padded along the way.
Too many things we truly value
wars and sports and celebrity
diverting the course of funding.

Too much noise in the law's conceiving,
too much agenda,
a dearth of grieving.

Far too many *can'ts* when a worker
wants to say, *I can.*

Too many rants when a worker
took off on conscience, dared and ran.

Too many scoldings when protocol
is duly breached.

Too many casualties of neglect
washed up on Eclipse Beach.

Time was when I believed change
could come in increments.

It can, though rarely in time
for the child who needs it.

Now I believe in revolution,
the only force strong enough
to decimate foul tradition at its root.

If what kills children
is only partially destroyed,
it grows new strangling weeds.

And so, I leave my files to their dust
and fate,

lubricate my rusted hinges,
swing open this work cage gate,

and march myself into retirement,
which for me shall be
a meeting with my inner authority.

I will take my assignment with newborn glee,

and sniff the subtle wind of my community
for aroma I should follow,
until I find a few simple souls
with hearts of courage
to do the thing a child needs,
in that very same moment the child bleeds,

no excuses, no misdirection.

We of meager means and salty predilection
will join hands,

walk into the burning building,
somehow find the child,
bring her out.

Turning round to face the flames,
we will die to put them out.

Our souls the seeping sieve,
we will die before we let
this burning live.

INTRODUCE YOURSELF

On the first day, she writes her name
in fine form in white chalk
on the licorice colored blackboard.

Good Morning, class, she says,
pointing to her name on the board:
I am Ms. Taylor.

She spends that first day telling stories
of her wonderfully imperfect childhood.

Her students respond with a hesitant
blend of wit and bashful silence.

On the second day, a small child
strides to the front,
picks up some chalk and writes:

My name is Acacia.

On the third day, a wispy one
comes to the board and writes:

My name is Nathan.

This continues by the day...
seemingly without conversation,
a new child stands and walks
and writes and declares a name.

The walls grow lush with vines of testimony
written in washable script.

That's not all that happens.

As the names begin to fill the board,
the children start to reach beyond
name and pronounce themselves
more completely:

I am the defender of my territory.

My Love maintains the peace.

I will never betray my family.

My heart's pool has no bottom.

Your stories are safe with me.

My every step is toward a better world.

The writing escapes the blackboard,
takes over the walls in a thick ivy of exclamation.

All because she introduced herself.

LA PREGUNTA

La pregunta:
Por que hacemos esta cosa.
Porque.

Por los que lloran en la noche.
Por los que sueñan por la mañana.

Por la luz dentro del dolor.

Por los corazones que transportan
fealdad y belleza.

Por el rio que corre entre cada niño,
un rio con hambre por almas florescentes.

Y porque hoy se casa
con ayer y mañana.

Y porque el cielo
y la tierra estan mirando.

Y cuando el pajaro
canta de felicidad,
los niños oyen.

Y cuando podemos ver
la sonrisa en el sol
al primer momento del dia,
podremos creer que
todo es possible para ella quien
tiene Fe.

Y cuando la bella luna dice,
Mirame, mirame.
No tengan miedo.

Tengan paciencia, como yo.
Los niños son arboles.
Un dia que viene, altos.
Pero este dia, pequeños y en sus manos.

Y cuando nos veamos en el future,
podremos decir:
En este dia, yo di
todo lo que soy a este niño,
ahora un hombre,
un arbol alto
quien besa cielo.

*This poem came to me in Spanish originally, as imperfect
as is my Spanish. I then shared with a close Spanish-
speaking friend and *legendary* educator the English words
that I intended for the Spanish version to accurately
represent. He graciously corrected the Spanish version for
me. The English version follows.

THE QUESTION

The question:
Why do we do this thing.
Why.

For those who cry in the night.
For those who dream in the morn.

For the light inside the pain.

For the hearts transporting
ugliness and beauty.

For the river that runs between every child,
a river hungry for flowering souls.

And because today marries
yesterday and tomorrow.

And because the sky
and the earth are watching.

And when the bird
sings of happiness,
the children are watching.

And when we can see
the smile in the sun
at day's first moment,
we can believe that
all is possible for she
who Believes.

And when brilliant moon says,
Look at me, look at me.
Do not fear.

Have patience, as I do.
The children are trees.
One day to come, towering,
this day, small and in your hands.

And when we see each other in the future,
we can say:
On that day, I gave
all that I am to this child,
now a man,
a tall tree
who kisses sky.

This is the English version of the preceding Spanish poem.

A PURE MOTIVE

He writes the words as a conclusion to his
self-evaluation report:

This is why I teach...

We believe criminals crawl out
of the woodworks.

We say they are a separate breed.

No.
They crawl out of childhood,
kin to the best of us.

Our young who we abandon
greet us later in wearier skin.

Their smirk is borrowed
from previous wearers of longer femur,
thicker conclusions,
bone plates through with transformation.

Their idea of limitation is drawn
from rancid well water of grown folk,
minds gone stale and bordered.

Their self-regard drips of sour sludge
from stalactites seeping down
inside our cavernous pessimism.

They suckle the teat of our gloom.
Those who hunt us do not materialize
like condensation on the drinking glass.

They become. Steadily.
A disordered calligraphy
drawn in slurred lines
ushered by our nervous tremors.

There comes a point when a frightened
soul must take a stand.

And so, before too many poisoned minds
lock up our young with cryptic ciphers,
I will steal their alphabet,

drown their social ideas
in the mangrove swamps,
where they can become detritus,
as is their only merit.

A long sojourn along prayer flag roads
on blustery mountain sides
brings me to a cave of blackened roof,
distal ashy fire illuminating
dancing figures on the walls.

Here is where I draw my conclusions.
Against this chalky rock, I practice
my drawing strokes.

I begin a novice,
leave not yet a master,

come down from the heights
to write a feel good story
into flesh and bone
of these early prophets each.

I strip ancient sinker cypress
lifted from swamp and bog,
now hard and heavy,
perfect for a writing instrument
that will not break.

I unroll sheets of bamboo paper.
With fledglings by my side,
we write together, stride for stride.

We become florid rhythm,
our strokes take to the page,
soak the fibers until

a rebellious vocabulary spills out,
a stunning mural in bright relief.

Because I have not let the false translators
dictate this long Love letter to our young,
these adolescent seekers leave behind
the contaminants that breed
in wet dank despair.

Now they have an entire manuscript
fit to publish to a world of readers,
a market famished for their genius composition.

Stained bamboo lodges in their teeth,
they grin goofy nonetheless.

This is why I teach.

BUSTING SCHEMAS

His conscience shows up in his dreams
as a drill sergeant berating him for this tendency
to see his students through stereotypes:

Is your corpus callosum finished
passing nonsense back and forth yet?

Myths run through that curtain,
mice scurrying nowhere,
leading you everywhere
but to understanding.

Choose a hemisphere,
discover its full stash of notions,
then select the other,
become friends with what it whispers.

Once you have become acquainted with the
persona of shadows, you can tease out the light.

Then the veil splitting your brain as a
mischievous membrane can be free to be a bridge.

Your epiphanies can cross back and forth
after partying on both sides.

This is better than when your rascal misbeliefs
darted between rationale and passion,
your fear patrolling the crossing place,
a hairy rebellious troll.

Seeing a young life clearly...
requires this kind of meditation.

BE WATER

Since she Loves the ocean,
her sister suggests a way for her
to relate to the defiant youth:

Be water.
Seep into the creases of his stone resistance,
expand into the crystalline
of your most beautiful nature.

Burst him open,
let him weep into fragments and shards,

that he may be made whole again.

Let his granite crumble,
his agate ore be revealed.

Let him return to sand
and discover how it feels to be
finely crushed coral,
Lovingly bedded into silt
by boundless affections of the sea.

Be water to him.
Let him return to the sea.

I WADE DEEPLY

She writes a poem in response
to her sister's urging:

I wade uncertain into cold broad sea
at foot of naked dawn.

This child's life rises around my ankles,
clenches tighter with every timid
step I take.

I, steadily sinking into sediment others
have laid down inside his heart.

Two realities exist in this water:

The one above.
The one beneath,
where organic neglect steeps and grows.

I leave his shoals,
wade unknowing into his wide waters.

Shelves exist beneath his surface.
At any step, I might encounter one,
plunge down into his deep,

suddenly come face to face with
the shadows and strange creatures
who inhabit his dark,
untouched by the light of Love.

Surely they are there,
those creatures,

those misunderstood things
that we call monstrous,
swimming in his abyss.

I wade in his waters.

I get wet,
dampened at the hem of my own heart,
when perhaps I would rather remain
dry and farther up on the shore.

His life is most truly lived out there,
in the deep where he treads water

with a rowdy school of peers.

Sometimes their bared teeth
I take as mockery,

that is, before I see the foreboding
fin sweeping swiftly toward them
in the waves.

Then I am reminded that their bared teeth
are the horrified grimace of lambs
at the mouth of the opened gate
we should have closed on our shift
that does not end.

And now the wolves descend from the hills,
all burl and brawn,
salivating at the opportunity to snatch
such a trembling and vulnerable flock
while still young.

And now the night owls cry an early alarm,
for it is not near dusk, but rather fat of day,
yet so brazen are these predators.

They close in on a prey whose shepherds
would rather not
wade in the water.

And so, I gather whatever kindling lies
scattered across the floor of my courage.

I light a fire, a torch, a brave candle
of faith and fortitude

that cannot be doused by such a thing
as treachery in the water.

I gather what I can,
take a deep breath,
submerge myself

into this child's deepness.

PRAYER OF CHOICE

If I have a prayer to keep me earnest
in this work often done in corners and shadows,
alongside cliff sides of fear and
steep slopes of shale loosening and lifting,

if I have a prayer to keep me earnest,
it is that I might find the will
to dissolve myself into this service of souls,

become smoke from compassion's candle,
achieve absolute annihilation of my ego
before this monumental task.

I pray that I may find the rough rock of reason
against which to shed my skin of insecurity,

that a hard and persistent rain will fall
to loosen the soil of my ideology,

that new understanding will receive the chance
to penetrate the surface of my *expertise,*

that a knowing light will infiltrate
the burrows where sleeps my soul,

a light so undeniable and burning
that my mind will be bleached
of all I thought I knew,
making way for a fresh tablet to be inscribed,
one whose words never completely
settle in the stone.

I pray for the vagrancy of my devotion
to find a lasting home,
perhaps in the nest that is my purpose revisited
daily, hourly, by the moment.

I pray to become a beacon atop a lighthouse
on the hill of humility,

forever looking up in admiration at this
vast array of children strewn across the sky,

that they might always locate North Star
shining through my nothingness,

and remember their way onward
to a glory that they own,

and when August days
burn a hole in my unsure chest,
leaving a geyser of ambivalence
to come gushing out,

and I doubt, pout, reconsider whether
I shall tread this road for another year,

I pray for a tear
that would fall from the heavens,
penetrate the abiding mist,
splash over my aching,
make all things clear,
brush me with a whisper
to leave with a child:

Be still, my beLoved.
I am near.

BUREACRACY

I dreamt one night
that I was a requisition form for services
one of my youth clients dearly needed.

I was a floating waif,
a wispy sheet of desires
tattooed in printed words describing
what *one child's life* required.

I drifted down a dark hallway,
staring up at blinking popping fluorescent lights.

Moving past co-workers in conversation,
I caught a downdraft,
landing on the first of a long series of desks,
where I awaited a signature from each.

After leaving the caseworker's hands,
I landed in the supervisor's basket.

She was on vacation, so I remained
for seven and one half days.

Next, the desk of the assistant program manager.
She had issues with a certain omission
from my text boxes and sent me back.

Eventually I made it to the unit manager,
where I stayed for a week while she
caught up on backed up work.

The unit administrator was embroiled in a crisis,
so I remained on her desk for two weeks.

My paper was yellowing and stained
when I reached the program manager,
who misread my print and sent me
in the wrong direction.

After correction, I came at last
to the chief operating officer,
who left me with her secretary
for another two days.

My stay with the chief of staff was brief,
only because he had me stuffed into his hands
while he was distracted.
He signed me without even reading me.

The assistant director passed me on,
having forgotten to sign,
so I came back again.

A couple of months after the beginning

of my sojourn, I was graced
by the deputy assistant director,
who exclaimed that I was a high alert priority.

The deputy director must not have thought so,
since I remained there a week.

At last, I was in the hands
at the top of the tower:
I was approved by the director.
I was legitimate!

Lo and behold,
just before I was returned to the caseworker,
ready to perform life saving things
for a youngster whose life hung
delicate on the vine,

a new administration took over.

All requisitions were now on hold
and under review.

I FIND MY SACRED LAKE

I find my Sacred Lake. I call my ancestral tribe of
sacred servants: All you healers, mystics,
medicine women and men, teachers, nurses,
doctors, shamans, holy ones, warriors. All of you
who pour out your blood on the fragile grass of
lives, who surrender your comforts for the chance

to comfort a soul in despair. Together, this healing prayer, we share:

I care... to be human... I won't let this mantra leave me. I won't let this moment take me, break me. I am ember waiting to be flame, waiting to warm these shivering masses. Oh Grace, ignite me again.

My heart is so many things: a lake rippling in the breeze, panting for shore, for safety, security, mine, theirs. My heart a dream of how beautiful this world can be. My heart the suffering of vulnerable ones huddled on the Trail of Tears. My heart an open valley, the lushness growing there, families gathered, verified, dignified.

My heart these endless memories of when we were intimate in sacred ways, when we sat by the fire and gazed upon illuminated faces, seeing straight into their souls, discovering their true nature, naked of the mask. My heart a Love letter to the world, punctuated passionately, drafted by candlelight in the storm, sealed by the wax of my concentrated tears.

My heart this mantra, pouring out endlessly, staying me in a place of Hopeful urgency, of Calm immediacy, shepherding voices to graze their own organic power and reach.

I wash my face in Sacred Lake. I clean my wounds in Sacred Lake. I fortify my courage at Sacred Lake. I remember my Divine Power at Sacred Lake. I forgive my trespasses and my trespassers at Sacred Lake. I fill my hunger, quench my thirst at Sacred Lake. I renew my Faith at Sacred Lake. I release my Love at Sacred Lake. I find myself at Sacred Lake and journey forward, my soul and service both vessels forever holding my Sacred Lake.

Woodpecker taps out the code for Peace. I open my chest and transcribe the truth. Cardinal and bluebird color my moment. I brush my imagination with their wondrous paint. I stop and smell an orchid, and realize orchid has stopped to smell me. So I bathe in the fragrance of a kinder meadow, wave smoke of sweet grass over my body. I become incense, Sun lights me. I burn, curl, and rise to the altitude where I cannot be touched by human cruelty and coldness.

I am warm sky, eagles draft me, we trade vision, I see my quarry: Harmony and Bliss in the midst of this soul service. I melt my walls of fear in a furnace of caring, daring to transform into an even Greater tool for human kind. Still glowing, my steel bends into an unbelievable Force, my glass polishes into a crystal face.

I kiss Bliss, Bliss kisses back... In this land of many wolves, I civilize the pack. I lead us to my Sacred Lake, where, heads bowed in collective *Namasté*, we stare deep into the clear reflection and see our purpose shimmering on the watery plate:

We were born to serve this Humanity. Caring is our calling. Soul service is our fate.

I find myself at Sacred Lake.

URGENT OATH

This is what she tells her seminar audience:

As I sat in the lunchroom just after our latest
assembly over our latest act of violence,
I scanned the faces and conversation of my
colleagues,

earnest souls caught in a drone of complaint
about the conditions of their profession,
and the pocked clamoring for something more.

As I worked to translate their sentiments
into a magic tonic that might hydrate
each of us back into plump vinery,
I became aware:

Most of my colleagues were consumed
with their jobs and thus without sight
for the children.

They were literally
not seeing the children.

In chills, I feared I might have already
caught this contagion.

I retreated immediately into a low murmur
of promises.

I gave myself an urgent oath
that began with what I cannot do:

I cannot teach them without touching
the dreams they stow away.

Somehow, I must call up something
old and wise within me,
and let it touch them.

Their hearts are bored and lonely land,
sorrow soaks the ravines of their cognition.

I must touch them in gentle ways.
I must locate something new inside myself,

some just born butterfly,
and loose it to flutter over to
where they tremble.

If that delicate thing of wings can land
somewhere near the perimeter
of their safety zone,
they might let me in.

I cannot trespass.
I need to become invited,
a neighbor bringing over their favorite dish,
not the nosy neighbor all up in their
private business.

The neighbor grateful that this child
has moved in next to me,
into my classroom,
my caseload,
my life,
my Love.

I should build a swing
hung from the fattest limb
of my tallest, strongest tree,
out in my best-groomed yard,
before my terrace cleaned and brightened
with baskets of crepe myrtle and iris.

I should welcome this child
to swing on the joy-making machine
I have built in my untamed yard.

I have to find a way to let him in.

My colleagues bash at times
with bricks and stones
on his doors and windows.

They form a desperate gathering
of authority circling his assaulted house,

calling attention to all his neighbors
that he is a troubled thing,
a menacing worrisome thing,
and won't he just let us in?

But we won't let *him* in,
and letting is where our bonding begins.

When *we* let down our hinge-rusted gate,
when *we* decide we will not abandon him
in our deepest heart,
this is when we touch our fate.

For when his nervous skin

receives the rippling air
of our door swung open wide,

he becomes invited.
He now gets to choose:

*do I take this hand,
and will I bruise?*

No,
I cannot teach them without
touching them emotionally.

I cannot stand across
the cloud crowned canyon
and yell, come to me!

What child would step out onto nothingness
without a blatant bridge?

I must be the one to harness my soul
to rising sun,

vault across the great expanse,
to land on his side
of being in this world.

I must come to him,
risk my heart on him,
make a blood oath that we
shall rise and fall together.

How can I teach them
and not Love them?
What paradigm is this?

How can I guide and counsel,
having never brought them near
my humanness?

I must introduce him to the story
of how I became me.

Others often harden
when they should soften,

pitter patter
when their best should matter,

teeter totter,
that's why surrender got her,

look away, look away
as young girl cries, look at me!

Not me.
I will Love them,
so I can learn them,

learn them,
so I can Love them,

so they can,
having been Loved,
learn,

having learned
Love.

THE LAST STRAW

The last straw came
when I showed up at the staff meeting
with toilet paper sticking
out of the heel of my pumps,

a humiliating trailer
on much less than my wedding day.

To top it off, a corner of my skirt
was hitched up in the back,
stuck in the waistband of my hose,
revealing my caboose in all its glory.

This, on a day of course when I had worn
my tattered Minnie Mouse panties no less.

They were a gift from my niece,
who if she had been there in that moment,
would have been on the floor howling
and crying with laughter,
along with every one of my co-workers,
including my supervisor
and her ten-year-old son,

who of course just *had* to choose that day
to get suspended from school.

And I'm just warming up...

I drove to work that morning with
the gas cap dangling from the side of the car
as I raced to not be late.

You see, I ran over my daughter's formerly
AWOL pet frog as I backed out
of the garage.

I heard the squish just as I turned
on the radio.

I thought the squishing sound
was signal static,
until I heard the most blood curdling scream
come from my daughter,

followed by her hideous death stare
directed at yours truly.

We held the impromptu funeral
in the backyard as my daughter
prayed out loud for God to please forgive
her *murderous mother*.

Finally, I left for work,
applying mascara in the rearview mirror
as I turned the street corner,
hit a pothole and stabbed a streak
of black cosmetic across my forehead.

At the stoplight, I thought I would be safe
to put on some lipstick.
That's when the dump truck behind me
blasted its horn to alert me to the green light.

I shrieked at the blast,
jarring the lipstick up my nose.

I now looked just a hair shy of insane.

At the staff meeting,
once my backside was covered
and the toilet paper removed,
and after the laughter died down
into fits and spurts,
my supervisor asked me with a face
near to bursting whether I had any more
outcomes to share with the group.

We never did manage to conduct
a serious meeting that day.

Before I could crawl under my desk and die,
my husband called to inform me that
it was raining and our dearly departed frog
had floated up to the surface in the yard,
and could I come home and comfort
our child, because *she sure was upset*,
and *I* was good at those kinds of things.

That was the last straw.

The next day, I told work I was leaving
the planet and would return
when I was human again.

I told my husband not to call me
even once if he valued his well-being.

I checked into a resort,
got a deep tissue massage,
then a Swedish massage,

a hot stone massage,
followed by a pedicure, manicure,
body wrap, scalp massage, and Jacuzzi.

I ate strawberries and chocolate in bed
to a series of old romance movies.

I listened to Italian operatic promises,
and at night I cried at the beauty
of the full moon set in a clear blue black sky.

I ordered room service when *I* wanted,
soaked myself silly in bubble baths,
went on long walks in tall woods,
wrote Love letters to my closest friends,
and joined some children playing stickball
in the street.

I picked wild flowers for myself,
and sang unabashedly with morning birds.

When *my soul* was satisfied,
I checked out of the resort,
amazed at what it felt like having
taken care of *me*.

I charged this whole affair with myself
to the account we kept for rainy days,
the one my husband pilfered from
for his golf habit which paid him in
nothing but curses and bogies.

I had come to realize that if I am going to
do this work of serving those in need,

I had better be willing every once in a while
to go crazy Loving myself,

lest crazy come and carry me away.

In the end, beLoved frog was laid to rest properly.

A stand of sunflowers grew
from that very ground.

As for me, I've managed to keep my bloomers
under cover and my head above
life's wild waters.

I've also learned I can do this work.
I just need a little self Lovin' sometimes.

NEW LANGUAGE

She stayed after school.

Dear child was only 14 when
she came into my office that first day
with eyelids at half mast,
her spine bowed as a sapling
beside wind-blown sea.

As she poured out her story,
catching, hitching, sobbing,
I realized we had made her a bag lady...
All of us.

All over her body she wore the layers
of what we had told her
all her life she was:

at risk, delinquent, troubled, poor,
learning disabled, oppositional, angry,
resistant, unworthy, pitiful,
unfortunate, special needs,
abused, neglected, abandoned.

We had woven a litany of shame
into her frayed composition.

She wore each of these labels
as a piece of clothing,
piles of burlap and grime
concealing her true nature,
stifling her ability to breathe.

The ensemble was enormous.

In a flash of awareness it came to me
that I could not truly *see* her
through her stacks of rejection.

Neither could she see herself.
The labels had become her stash
of self-slur and denunciation.

She pushed these invectives around
like a grocery cart out in front of her,
forming a barrier against the world.

She had become skilled at recognizing
put-downs scattered around her home,
in the streets, at school.

She would pick up that litter,
put it in her overburdened cart,
make it hers.

She was hoarding stained trinkets
from society's gutters,
stuffing them into her awful identity,
fiercely protecting her putrid pile of self ideas
from anyone who tried to take an item.

This dear child had burrowed deep into
the accumulation of our insults,
and now was beating us to the punch.

She was calling herself these things
before we could spit them at her.

I think it hurt her less to be splattered
with our judgments if she had already
judged herself with the same un-anointing oil.

She was a soaking wet creature
hiding beneath a mound of humiliation.

She was hiding from all of us,
from everything,
most of all, from herself.

I realized nothing was going to ever change
for her.

She would spend the rest of her life
scavenging filth as a bag lady unless
someone helped her put down her load.

It had to be me.

I would be that one steady ground for her,
that one solid place,
enduring force,
unending belief in her world
of shifting sand and sweeping shadows.

I would be that sanctuary of stillness.
I would be her leaning tree.

At first, she lashed out at me,
a mother animal protecting her den.

I had to go on a quest for new language,
a different logic.

I had to convince her that what she prized
was in fact her enemy,
that what she truly needed,
she saw instead as foe.

I offended her greatly,
and still I endured.

I said, Honey, we are going to work together
to take off all these old clothes,
to unpack and discard all this trash.

We're going to teach you how to reject

the garbage people throw at you.
You're going to learn to see beauty again.

And most of all, I promise you this:
I am going to change.
I am going to learn a new language for you.

My understanding was rising.
We, her caretakers and authorities,
had been persistently waiting for her
larvae state to transform into
a winged attraction.

Instead, what she needed was for us to
look at her with new eyes,

to see the butterfly morphing inside her chrysalis
so we could tell her stories of who she was,
latently.

She needed our bridge to her Love's affair.

The work was difficult.
She had no attraction for labels
that told of her value.
She did not want them in her cart,
did not think she could trade them for
useful things on the streets.

We took long walks together
so she could learn how to gather goodness.

At first, she bypassed all manner of beauty,
seemed not to even notice the glimmer.

She almost salivated at the pollution, though,
swerving toward it like a hound
at the rabbit's hole.

When we passed by storefront windows,
she never looked at her reflection.

When I asked her to,
she broke down something terrible.

She said:
I do not know that stranger.
She terrifies me.

All this while, I worked at changing.
I needed to learn to list her good things first.

I came up with new names for her.
I shared them with my colleagues,
friends, and family,
forcefully.

I was determined to plant new seeds.

When she struggled with a school exam,
I called her *a rare and priceless learner.*

I talked about her anger as a molten fire
that she would smelt into gold.

I learned to call her Magnificent, Majesty.
I called her Oshoon.

I called her great, glorious, glowing,
even if I had to convince myself first.

Before, I had been her bag lady helper.
Now, I was her beauty chaperone.

I kept reciting the mantras of her worth
to myself at night, to her at day.

She kept inserting old language,
the slings and stonings
with which she was comfortable.

I kept erasing her obsolete alphabet.

One day, we stopped before a storefront window.
She stared at her reflection.
I asked her what she saw.

She said:
I see a beautiful stranger.
She scares me to death.

In that moment...
I knew change was on the cusp.

ONE TEACHER

Every child deserves to fall in Love
with one teacher.

Every child deserves to have one adult,
beyond the walls of home, see her beauty.

One person crowned with wisdom
who says to the child,
you are special in my eyes.

One glorious soul who walks
hand in hand with the young
down their imperfect path,
believing in them with every step.

One glistening rainbow whose rich colors
reflect its celebration of youthful spirit,
tender sensitivities, awesome possibilities.

One fantastic waterfall
whose fluid curtain is a security blanket
of joyful, painful, compassionate tears
cascading into the heart river of that child.

One brilliant sunrise who brings hope
and optimism to gray and stony childhood days.

One gorgeous sunset whose autumn panorama
reminds the child that he walks
into a fruitful night,
walks closer to a tomorrow
of new flame burning bright.

Every child deserves to fall in Love
with one teacher.

Every teacher deserves to be Loved by one child.

One surging tide of life's potential,
ocean wide, a smile inside,
a flame alit against the dark,

fed by her teacher seeing her, giving for her,
releasing her on a magic carpet ride
toward her life's purpose,

a gallant stride past her current days,
to her future glory rays.

Every child deserves to fall in Love
with one teacher,

Who would step before the train
of adult foolishness and sacrifice herself,
so the child might ride into his own waterfall,
her own sunrise, his own sunset,
her own rainbow...

Oh, such a teacher,
a hopeless optimist who chants to herself:
If I can invite the light of
a child dim and grim,

If I can quiet the clamor,
awaken the spark,
shoo the locusts,
shush those who doubt,
find what is not seen...

an optimist who imagines *if I can,*
so she does.

I know a teacher
who will *always* be a teacher,
and our child-Love for her will always reach her
wherever she may be.

For, a child who Loves a teacher
becomes a mighty reacher,

and a teacher who Loves a child,
well... God Bless that priceless teacher.

Her Love will return to her multiplied
a million fold and thousands will beseech her,

for she is a once in a lifetime gift
for the child who desperately
needs her to be what she is:

So much more than a teacher.

Written for my favorite teacher, Roberta Cocking, to honor
and celebrate her legendary Love and devotion to our
becoming ones.

RENEWING A SOUL

The worker has grown weary
of her co-worker's sourness and bigotry
toward peers, the community, even the young,

and yet, she cares for him,
and so, beneath a maternal oak
on the lawn by the building at noon,
she speaks up:

This is not my anger for you,
rather a Love tree blossoming in winter.

The lash I wield grows from my own
dark marsh boiling.

In doing this... this scolding,
I hope mist might rise from agony,
become a revelation of self that frees me.

And so...
You are hard stone turned inside itself,
a petrified tree root gnarled beyond recognition.

Jesus wept, and you told him to get over it.
He spilled his heart over human sin.
You told him to stop being so sensitive,
stop Loving so much.
Thank God he did not.
He knew he was born for this.

Mohammed met Moses, Krishna, Buddha
in the courtyard to protest a stoning.
You ridiculed them for caring too much,
and for believing they could change the world.
Fortunately, they were deaf to your frequency.

Socrates met the Egyptian philosophers
for tea and some sweet bread.
You told them to go home,
that they thought too much,
over-analyzed everything.

Thankfully, they ignored you.

Had they amputated their intelligence
and retreated from your judgmental scorn,
this world would have diminished that day.

You are not the way men should be.
You are a bee in the way of men.

Small, agitated, pestering flier,
you mistake flesh for a flower.
Seeking to feed from dignity,
sacrilege should not be your meal.

Burying your stinger in an enemy
that is in truth your own beLoved.

You confused, barren land,
sufferer of dreams born in putrid water,
come out of that stench at last,
dry your wings on licking sun.

Her taste finds you salted turgidity,
but when she is done suffering your foul flavor,
world erupts with blemishes,
a sign of healing,

clouds stop hoarding their water,
madmen are listened to just long enough to share
a priceless truth,

children squealing because they are not seen,
stop,

in dank corners they realize light has broken
through. Eyes for seeing come with it.

Now, they have a chance to be human.
What makes them beautiful blazes on their skin.
They straighten their spines, walk out into day.

Because your blindness has been killed,
because your knotted heart is blown open,
all living things are free to breathe again.

REMEMBER YOUR PROMISE

Sun rises to warm this earth.
I rise to warm these child souls.

I burn to serve the precious gem
still glowing from its incubation bath.

No breath within my body
is free from this vocation.

No single heartbeat not enlisted
in this obligation.

I am grown only in the degree
to which I bless our growing ones.

If we are human,
where is our humanness?

In a child's eyes.

If children look upon

us and see a safe land to enter,
only then may we know
that which we so prematurely assume:

that we are human *kind*.

WHAT THE PEACE PIPE SPEAKS

The following is not a factual representation of Diné culture, but a poetic imagination of aspects of this community emerging from conversations between the author and tribal members.

Four thousand seasons ago, in what is now the Arizona desert, a young Diné (Navajo) man sat on a large sandstone boulder. The sun stood at full height. The desert slept. He stood up to speak to several spirits who had come from another time; a time that greets us now. The spirits were thirsty, not for water, but for wisdom. Their own time was barren of such things as what they sought, here, with this young man before them. He rose. He spoke these words:

My people smoke the peace pipe. We have, for as long as the sun has risen across our lands and warmed our faces. We come together in a circle because a circle is life's Love song to itself. Love flows better that way. We sit because this brings us closer to Mother Earth, close where she can whisper her wisdom into our stubborn ears.

We sit in a circle and smoke the peace pipe, each wanting lip touching that wooden vessel, through which Spirit flows and takes us to the Great Meadow in our mind. We do this thing before a journey, in the face of danger, or when mystery blows into our lives, a gray cloud dancing on our horizon.

In the pipe, we use tobacco that has been blessed. Many times, we also use other herbs for their sweet taste or pleasing scent; herbs such as sweetgrass, cedar, white sage, bearberry leaves, spearmint, and red willow bark. We gather, we sit, we smoke. We take spirit flight. We leave here, this chaos place where touchable things are illusion and shadows howl like coyote through the day. We go on spirit wings to the Great Meadow in our mind.

For each of us, this meadow is its own unique beauty. It is a place where the water runs clear, the wind brings good word, the Earth is black and fertile. Trees are plenty; grass whispers; eagles patrol a deep blue sky. Most of all, in this meadow, we find ourselves; we find our Essence. That Essence has been a wild horse loosed from our hold, un-tethered and roaming as we stumble through our practical lives. But here, beside the crystal water, where every living thing speaks and we can hear, we find reunion with our Essence. We sit with our Essence after approaching it slowly, careful not to scare it away. For wild things will always seek freedom, and this world that men have created is a prison of daunting magnitude.

We sit with our Essence, it calms us immediately. We begin to experience its shimmer as words painting themselves across our consciousness. The portrait is brilliant and expansive, its colors so powerful they combust, become clouds, heavy, swollen, pregnant. Those clouds rain, we stand beneath the shower, become painted in the glory of our own truth. We call this pipe the peace pipe because it is only by traveling on the journey of self-discovery that one may attain peace. Truth is that destination.

My people are teachers. We smoke the pipe also when we prepare for the journey of learning, a journey that binds us to the students, like corn to husk, seed to root, sun to light. You have been told that my people smoke the pipe to bring an end to war. You have been told wrong. What we do, more than anything, does not end war. It prevents it. Internally. By visiting our Essence, we are reminded of why we are here. Why we were born teachers. We remember the truth of our nature—that we burn for growth and rage at the dying of the soul.

Our Essence scolds us for forgetting that the sacred bond between teacher and student is formed in the mist of transformation and humility. That to be a true teacher we must become a student of the student. That we must invite the student to release her greatness, become her own teacher.

We must fold our ego into silence and stroke the embers of a quiet child soul into a proud symphony of flame. For fire is not so much destructive, as you have been told. It is reconstructive. It takes away the pollution of life and beckons new growth from the soil of a resurrected garden. In teaching we must be willing to bleed, to die of our old selves and become new in every student. They will carry our spirit forward in their living. Their life shall be our offspring. But to truly teach, we must shed old skin. Every moment of every day, we must begin again.

Our elders told us that one day the world would change. That the noise of *civilization* would drown out the sweet, tender song of the human spirit. And in that dark dusk a crisis would be born. Children would die away in great numbers, and in spirit long before in body. Our elders told us that blind men would seek to end this plague by spewing forth more *civilization*—more noise.

The crisis would continue walking toward the Great Death. Our elders told us that there would be one medicine and one medicine alone for this plague: Teachers. Brave souls who would somehow recover the old ways. They would come together, sit in a circle, smoke the peace pipe, find the courage to flee their false selves and sojourn to their own Divine Meadow for a reunion with their truth. Here, they would sit beside their Essence and remember the reason for their Love, their passion, their deep ache, their many tears. Here they would summon courage, walk back through the woods to a wanting world... and they would teach.

This is what I have been told, by the elders, and by my own spirit. More important this day is not

what I have been told. More essential is this:
What does *your* spirit speak to *you*?

The last words the young Diné spoke were:

May this day hold well my words, for I fear a
great dying is soon upon us. Still, I see the sun
has risen and is of a proud height at this moment.
There is more life to live. My heart beats with a
hopeful blood.

YOU ARE CHERISHED

She walks with a palsied limp,
is taunted as slow for her lisp
and scholastic tracking,
Loves wearing daisy prints,
tells fantastic stories to her pet retriever,
yet never utters a word
of these fables to others,

except to her mentor,
whom she adores.

She is a closed music box
playing concertos in private.

When the box is pried open,
it yawns silently,
gives up no song.

One afternoon by the lake,
she hugs her mentor
with a Love song:

Walking through life with you
is like holding hands with sunrise daily.

You lift me up on thermal ribbons.
You sew me with crystal light.

I cannot look away from you.
Disbelief tangos with gratitude
on the dance floor of my heart.

You bind my wounds with
the salve of your goodness.

You *see me* through my
layered thickets of imperfection.

Am I an excavation
your inner government grants?

Will you unearth all my pottery,
the shards of bowls,
tiny specks of spoons and ceremony,

evidence of my prior diet,
the stone toy I played with beneath
the drainage pipe of lonesomeness?

How long do you get to keep digging?
I hope at least until my bones
come up and bleach in blinding waves.

Use your hands for this meal.
Your utensils are useless,
but how I Love the dewy kindness
of your steep-striated fingertips.

Dig me deep,
excavate what I am into who you are:

a sunrise I hold hands with,
my superficial burned away
on your sizzling orb,
my elated soul aloft
from Earth so gladly.

CLEAN ENOUGH TO SERVE

She has been told terrifying things
about *those people* all her life.

Now she will be working with them.
serving them.

She makes a date with her fears,
sits down at the table where
prejudice has already been served,
and pours the wine of determination.

She can be heard mumbling to herself:

Truth is,
I am afraid of these children.

We attribute the horror of their internal poverty
to everything but our own prejudice.

We never bite open the rotten seed.
It is left to grow to allergen weed
across the careless expanse of fiscal seasons.

I need to bleed past the crust of comfort
and fill the vessels that matter, so far as peace,
shake the shudder, roil, creep of fear.

Humility is not my familiar yet.
My ego masquerades as sensitive soul wronged.
I scatter wings of flying things
who would approach,

heavy-handed batter at the sky,
whipped defense with reckless lash,
perimeter casualties more apparent
than those close at home.

Roam the roads, teacher,
find the stones, abandoned,
reason to stop and kick,
what of the progress to be made?

Even leathered lizards seek the shade.
The need though is for endurance,
and sharp will,
when sweat brims upon us.

Trespass first, on soil of soul,
then the pain.

After this, we learn the ways to abbreviate,
the shake, shudder, roil of dagger,
stab, swing, rake, claw, roar,
we have it now: the way.

Child defense barricades itself within
bricks and mortar, limed and grained,
stays mortar shells from the breach,
august ripening of this as twelve-moons pass
into revolutions numbering more than teens.

We come to grown,
and seek the stone,
to kick and stay us,
from the childish ways which gray us
to the colors we could touch.

Too much pain,
too strong the habits:
I am afraid,
you hurt me so deep,
how do I defend but to scream,
how do I avoid but to anger,
rage is the one thing whose flame
offers me protection from you
who hurt me,

now I take control, and hurt myself,
and all who trespass upon
or enchant my tethered soul.

See this madness?
Who can Love this way?
Tonight I cut the umbilicus
to lies that raised me.

This day, I blank the slate and raise the query:

What snap will loose the lock?
What force will send flying
this grounded flock?

What light will kiss freedom
into the breast of our humanity?

What nudge to send the boulder rolling?
What to unclench fearful fist of heart?

What light to thaw the frozen soul?
Which breath to release the bud?
Break open dams?
Seduce the grass to dance?

Whose first shy step forward
will commence this long romance?

I say mine shall be that step.

•

When she is sacredly inebriated
on this reckoning with
a lifelong dysfunction
in her way of seeing others,
she leaves the table,

and stumbles home, smiling.

She carries a new heart,
free of inhibition,
and clean enough to serve.

TRUE REWARDS

Who comes to walk among
the meek should not seek
reward in material creek.

In that water, fool's gold
shall be panned for eternity.

Those who drink from this,
fill mouths with deceitful water,
and die of thirst halfway home.

Seek instead the barley for your bread
in the mindful sight born of a higher state
that recognizes everlasting quiver
of human strands in nature's web.

Your riches live inside relationship,
invest in this and your returns will grow,
regardless the fickle swoons of commodity.

Locate the frequency at which beauty speaks
in the chambers of a dawning life.

Tune your instrument to this,
and you will have more than wealth,
you will have become wed to bliss,

and spilled your purse
over all who walk with you.

SPIRIT CHECK

After many nights of sleep disturbed,
she is ready.

She sits with her colleague over tea.

By the second cup,
she finds her courage.

She starts:

I know you are a good person
with a caring heart.

I know you are intelligent, skilled,
experienced after all these years.

But you are killing the light
in these young lives.

You are killing the joy in your colleagues.

Your attitude and energy dishonor
the legacy of your years of service.

•

She knows her colleague will react defensively.
She does, at first.

The reaction is a long litany
of merit and worth:

Nobody has put more into these youth
than I have.

I have sacrificed my health, income,
time with my family, and more,
to do this job.

I have put up with the dysfunctions
of this system,

endured daily crises and stress.

The youth don't appreciate
what I do for them.

More and more of them keep
flooding through the door,
broken, angry, alone.

My caseload grows higher,
my resources thinner.

I'm not a magician,
I'm not a miracle worker.

•

Facing this resistance, she tries again:

My dear, even your reaction
tells the story of your bitterness.

Do you not see how your resentment
stings the hearts of the ones
you claim to serve?

You cannot resent them and truly serve them,

cannot scorn them and still uplift them,

cannot make them trust you,
when you have no faith in them,

and all the knowledge you possess
is not reaching your co-workers.

You have shut the door of your compassion
in their startled faces.

They respect your insight and want
to come to you for mentorship,

but you drive them away with your vibe
that says, *don't bother me.*

The problem is, *you* no longer bother.
You do not bother to listen,
to learn, to teach, to grow.

Your emotions have calcified
in your chest.

You bring hardened feelings
to the office each day:

petrified wood that once was supple
and pliant but now is turned to stone
under the relentless heat and aridity
of your disillusionment.

You bring us this rock-wood
to place on our office hearth,

expecting us to receive it as kindling
for our morale.

You do not notice that its stony nature
puts out the flames and leaves us cold and drafty.

Then you complain about how you
are treated coldly.

You brought the chill that haunts your bones.

You have lashed hard plates of armor
onto your shield of self-defense.

You have forgotten kindness, warmth, gentleness.

You say you are no magician, but you are.
You have forgotten your magic chemistry,
lost your magic touch.

You lost your lust for giving the audience,
these children,
Joy.

You say you are no miracle worker,
but you are.

You have saved lives at the last moment.
You have changed the course of despair
into hopefulness countless times.

Perhaps you have lost the ability
to recognize a miracle where it grows.

Maybe you have missed the miracles
that live between agony and throes.

You've fallen in Love with your own misery,
and she is far from an unrequited Love.

She courts you back,
takes you on long walks of pessimism
and negativity.

When you return, you have no appetite for joy.

Once, you carried a sunny disposition.
The strains of this work weakened you,
and one day, you let your sun go down.

I believe it still exists.
It waits for you to find a reason to raise it,
and make sorrow a delighted dawn.

I care for you, but I am responsible
for these youth.

I am asking you to go home and pray this night,
for if you still find yourself stabbing children
with indifference and impatience,

if you continue slapping colleagues
with rancor and gloom,

I pray you will find the courage
and the grace to leave this work.

If you cannot stop hurting children
with your judgment and prejudice,

if you cannot join the work
at which your teammates toil,
and join it with a humble
open heart of ministry,

I pray you will summon the responsibility
to leave this work.

Only certain souls belong in this
great endeavor that swims inside
the fate of lives.

The youth we serve are boisterous,
but if you find yourself frustrated
at the constant darting about
of the hummingbird,

do not blame the hummingbird,
it is being what it is.

For stillness, go and find a tree,
and pray no wind kicks up.

If you cannot help but grieve this work,
please, leave this work.

We can never ever cleave this work
from the mores of Loving decency.

And please believe this work
deserves our excellence most urgently.

The most honorable servant finds a way
to become softened as she is wizened,
even as those around her harden.

She practices compassion as a daily
yoga against people's inflexibilities.

Please, I ask you,
go and be with yourself,
ask these questions and find your answers.

Remember, we have a special calling:
to walk with the wounded
and *do no further harm.*

•

She does not know if she has spoken
the right words, or if those words
have gotten through.

She is concerned that she has offended,
but is relieved she has been most true.

•

They sit again for tea.
During the first cup, redemption pours out:

I want to say that I have come to realize,
all you said to me was true.

I do not want ill spirit to be my legacy.
I really do cherish this service
and care about the lives I touch.

I did pray, and when I realized the harm
that I have done, my hardened heart
broke and died.

A new heart was born in me.
I feel new and whole again.
I will thank you for the remainder
of my life.

You have helped me to *see* myself.
I have made a choice:
I choose to learn and teach
and heal my wounds.

I choose to speak Lovingly,
to listen with compassion,
and to act bravely against the storm.

I choose grace and dignity
over stern intimidation,

humility over derogation,
beauty over ugliness.

I choose to act in Love
as I serve these youth.

I choose all of this because,
I choose this work.

A PRINCIPLED PRINCIPAL

She was a principal,
and principled.

She was a miracle worker,
tending to students, parents,
staff, administration, media,
community, and culture of the day,

sometimes losing hair and hospitality,
but never losing hope.

She was a persistent rebel,
determined to *Love them*,
even as *power* demanded her allegiance
to convention and not to Love.

She kneeled down each long day,
dug her fingers into the soil,
where she caressed them at their root.

Above ground, scarecrows frowned,
but all the flowers purred,

and the garden
clowned.

SETTING SONGBIRDS FREE

He fed his parakeets cracker crumbs
through the bars of their cage
as they pecked at his fingertips,
sometimes drawing blood.

He thought of his juvenile wards,
the *delinquents*.

Faithfully, he kept trying to feed them, too,
through the bars of their imprisonment.

Often, they drew his blood.

He learned quickly that he had to make
a decision about which was stronger:
their self-hatred and resistance,
or his resilience as a teacher/guide.

Not a discovery,
a decision.

He decided to believe more in what
he was born with
than what had been put into them:

his Purpose, over their acquired pollution.

He knew his devotion
was their absolution.

Each day, he fed his parakeets crumbs ⌐
through the bars of their cage.

He wondered what it took
for a songbird,
once caged,
to truly be free,

and lose its sharp beak
for drawing blood.

One day, he brought home a new bird,
older and proud,
fresh from freedom's plains.

The new bird spoke Lovingly
with the caged birds,
in a common language
known to those born to flight.

Before too long,
the caged birds lost their sharp beaks,
grew new down.

Seems that freedom
is a spirit eternal,
alive in the stories
of our true nature
that free birds pass around.

LETTER TO THE PRESIDENT

She was going to change careers,
until *this*.

She reads the young lady's letter
over yet again:

Dear Mr. President,

I've known terror in the cold bed
of my nervous sleep.

It crawls through my window,
puts frost on my floor,

bangs on the pipes,
and taps on my door.

I've known terror far too well.
Each day when I wake,
fear casts a brand new spell.

I know terror in my brother's face
as he slumps off to school,
not knowing whether he'll be
shot by a peer or snagged by fate.

I know terror in mom's sad eyes
as she serves me half a meal,

scared that she can't see half a dollar
coming her way,
to pay for the next half a meal
she'll serve to her children
to last a whole 'nother day.

I know terror in the hate
that targets my skin,
and the dirty desire
that prowls for my curves.

I know terror in the chill that spreads
through my nerves as the hopeless
trade gunshots through the night,
and I keep waiting for a bullet
to turn out my light.

I know terror in the hole in my chest,
where everyone's nasty ideas of me
bore through, before coming to rest.

I know it in not knowing whether
tomorrow I'll be put in the system
or kicked out of school
cause I *can't learn.*

I know it in the way grown folks
shoot disgust through their eyeballs at me
at church *as they pray.*

I know it in our naked school library
with hardly a book,

and all the supply money our state budget took.

I know it to lurch in the nook,
and in the cranny,
and in the hospital that turned away granny,
cause she had no insurance that day.

I know it in my neighborhood's
only insurance plan,
the one that says you folks are sure
to get the very last crumb,
and if you think we're gonna give
you what the good folks get,
you sure must be dumb.

Mr. President, I know you care a whole lot
about fighting bad guys you call terrorists,
say you'll chase them to the ends of Earth,

but can you please start in my city first?

I know terror that takes to the shadows
and leaps from my walls.

You go to war on terror to keep bad things
from happening, but my terror *lives*.
Bombs blow up around me every day.

Bad things
have perfect attendance in my school,
make every curfew at my house.

Mr. President,
you go to war overseas,
but please,
won't you go to war right here for me?

.

After reading this letter once more,
she copies it and mails it to the president,
the administration,
every single member of congress,
and every elected official she can think of.

She mails herself the letter twice a year.

And she goes out onto the field
to wage Love against the cold
that creeps through windows
and leaves frost on the floor.

WAKE AND BE WARRIORS

Wake this day and be warriors.
Wake, and feel the amber moon in your chest.

Solar face dances far away,
brings fire visions near.
Your soul is a fire dancer, *leap.*

Salmon swim toward spawning,
leaping impossible water staircases,
leap like this, with a spirit that will not be denied.

All that ails you this day
is also your medicine,
offered to you by a forest of compassion.

Drink.

Sully not the waters in complaint or lament,
leave that silt at the bottom for those
who choose to be bottom dwellers.
Drink the clear water that runs swift,
heal yourself inside Love's tonic.

Run like the fawns of spring,
surge into a magical allegory
that finds you in a meadow,
and all you desire abundant.

Wake this day your passion.
It has hibernated long enough.
Bring it out into the sun
and let light do what it does to dreams.

Wake this day your ancestors,
those of blood or spirit
who chase you toward your reason.
Let their desire for your life
lift you on high warm, currents.

Be an eagle, not a rodent scurrying
for its habitual den.

Be what drafts and sees all things.

Wake this day your ancient drum.
It has been sleeping in your heart.

Let your entire soul
play a sacred rhythm
on drum's awakened face.

Let the vibrations fall as ceremonial rain
inside your being.

Begin to dance,
this is feast day.
Gather your whole village
of breath and essence and emotion,
and dance in moonlight,
dance for spring,
dance for new beauty in your life.

Wake this day and be warriors.
Wake and feel the amber moon in your chest.
Let it pour its glowing molten power
through your percolating plains.

Let moonflowers grow in your life,
sacred stalks of Peace and Stillness
whose faces look like you
when you are in your groove
and floating, lotus caught in Light.

CHOOSE GOOD WATERFALLS

The young man puts his heart into words
along the margins of his favorite book.

The book and the words
will now be his gift to her:

Dear Miss,
please take good care of yourself.

I do not have many beautiful things in my life.
I would not want anything to happen to you.

Please take care of your heart.
I can feel you carrying my pain.

A heart can only hold so much.

Make sure you treat yours well,
you ask it to do so much feeling.

Laugh and cry each day,
sometimes both bring healing tears.

Sometimes, neither does,
but both break open the scars
that seal our souls,
leaving them tight and stiff.

Laughing and crying keep us open
and full of life.

Make sure to do the things that make you
feel good about yourself, as often as you can.

Learn how to Love who you are.
Make yourself safe on the inside,
even if your work doesn't always
make you feel safe on the outside.

Choose good waterfalls under which to stand.

You can't Love yourself properly unless
you shower yourself with people who see
your truest beauty flaming as a candle inside.

Those who Love you but cannot see you
are often careless with the way they breathe
in your direction, and blow your candle out.

Forgive yourself as often as you
disappoint yourself, so you can be free
to try again with new wings.

Learn new ways to call yourself *Beautiful*.
Practice letting hurtful people's words
and actions pass through you
as though you are not there.

Remember to breathe.
Turn off your brain when it gets too rowdy.

Lose yourself in good music
when all around you is awful noise.

Be an archaeologist,
dig for priceless treasures beneath the dirt.

Shine a light on ignorant conversation,
that way you won't trip and stumble
on karma in the dark.

Fill your mind with your favorite flowers,
don't wait for Love's bouquet.

Avoid clouds of human pollution
when you can't breathe your inner air.

Grow accustomed to spending time
and energy on your *state of being*,

invest in this stock that blesses
its investors miraculously,

pay the price for peace.

And know
that I pray deeply for your soul.
May it dance long and joyful
in its own sunlight,
that this world be blessed
by your fullest blossom.

IDEALISM MEETS TRUTH

In an early moment of a hiring interview,
the interviewer asks the young professional,
why do you wish to do this work?

Idealism smiles and cheerfully answers:

I just Love children and youth.
I want to do something to improve their lives.

I want to give back and help them
discover their greatness.

But will you die for this?

Idealism is startled speechless.

Will you die for this?
What I mean is, will you die *out of* your beliefs,
your values, your ways of seeing?

Will you die *out of* comfort, safety, security?
Out of expectations, impatience, ego?

Will you die *into* nakedness,
vulnerability, humility?

Will you die *out of* control and *into* surrender?
Die *out of* cultural superiority
and *into* cultural sacredness?

Die *out of* conformity and popularity
and *into* a revolutionary's solitude?

Die *out of* socialized identity
and *into* the Great Nothingness of service?

Will you die for this?

•

Long pause, and then idealism's response:

How much does this job pay again?

BAD SPOUSE, GOOD SPOUSE
(A BETTER WAY TO BUTTER YOUR BREAD)

Honey?

Yes, darling.

I can't sleep.

What is it?

I'm sorry to wake you, but I can't get this
little boy out of my head.

What is bothering you?

I'm just worried about where he's headed.

He's so angry.
His father is absent,
his mother detached.

He's being academically tracked
because of low test scores,
not showing up for school,
and violent behavior.

He has so much to offer.
He is a brilliant artist,
but no one encourages him.

He carves amazing images.
Unfortunately, he carves them
into his desktop and classmates' lockers.

He's wearing the same jeans he wore last year,
even though he's three inches taller.

I have a bad feeling that he is falling
into an unreachable hole,
that he is giving up on life.

He's just not getting any Love.

I'm feeling so limited in helping him,
a nervous premonition tugs at my chest.

When I leave work,
his life is following me to the car.

When I turn on the radio, his torment
is being played on every channel.

When I clear my mind, his conflict
keeps clouding my sky.

When I come home, his deniers
greet me at the door.

His bitterness curls my tongue as I eat,
his tears soak me as I shower.

And now, his nightmares have
invaded my dreams.

Wow, darling.
He sure has gotten to you.

He hasn't gotten to me.
His life has gotten to me.
We in his life, have gotten to me.

Darling, I just think maybe you're taking
too much responsibility on to yourself.

His life is not yours to save.
He needs to suck it up,
turn things around.

It's too bad he's not getting any Love,
but he can't let a lack of Love get him down.

Silence.

Morning comes.

Darling, I'm leaving for work.

Okay.

What, no goodbye kiss?

Suck it up, honey,
don't let a lack of Love get you down.

[alternate outcome]:

Wow, darling,
this boy's situation sure is wearing on you.

I can only imagine how being in the middle
of these difficult lives must affect you.

Especially being so restricted by
policies
liabilities
bureaucracy
politics
norms

I tell you what,
let's you and I together take some time
and talk about what we can do together
to help you feel less stressed by your work
and more empowered to make a difference.

I want you to pour it all out to me.
I want to understand better
the nature of your work.

And for right now, I want you
to rest peacefully.

So, know that I Love you,

I believe in you,
and together we're going to figure out
how to change this boy's life.

Honey, thank you so much for that.
I feel better already.
I Love you,
goodnight.

•

Morning comes.

Darling, please stop undressing me,
I need to get to work.
What did I do to deserve your
passionate affection this morning?

This? This is for the good Loving
you gave me last night.

POURING PURPOSE

She wanted to serve *that* community,
the one of which we are so afraid.

She was conflicted deeply,
echoes of her Loved ones' advice
and that of strangers boomed
with great industry through
the vulnerable theatre of her skull:

Are you sure you want to put yourself at risk?

One person cannot change the world.

Why not just put your Love into
your own children one day?

I'm just worried about your safety.

What about your retirement benefits?

You won't get rich doing that.

Your uncle has a "good" job for you.

Her heart was decomposing cabbage.
Whenever these discouraging thoughts
rampaged, her resolve wilted and stank.

Yet, in the absence of this cacophony,
her passion rang true,
confidence returned.

Knowing she needed stronger fortitude,
she went searching for inspiration.

She found it in a manuscript
of desert origins and distant times.

It was dulcet to her yearning.

It read:

Opportunity lies unseen in the dark.

Only the illumination of Purpose
reveals this cloistered mass.

We must project our true self,
our genuine destiny,
onto that shy plant in the corner
of blackened space.

Our greatness sits,
hot and boiling, in the vat
of our disbelief in self.

It could rampage through night
and lift the curtain on what may be,

but first, we must pour.

We must pour out our greatness,
heave our totality
onto the barely breathing fire.

Its flames will explode
into pillars of brilliance.

The timid plant will catch
both heat and light,
become fed.

Instantaneously,
when we cast our Divine reason
for living out across space,
we bring opportunity
out of the shadows,
and trembling sprout
becomes a giant tree,
becomes a forest,
becomes entirety.

Our purposeful life

has always been before us.
It is our vision that has failed.

We deceived ourselves
into thinking our purpose
was nowhere to be seen.

Purpose is always before us.
Like a small child,
it aches for our recognition.
It cannot believe
we cannot see its grandiosity.

It, the canyon of ten thousand miles.
We, the ant at its edge treading
in fretful circles wishing to encounter
something beyond mundane.

No one owns the manuscript,
the container,
the map,
to the hidden treasure
of our destiny.

It is free of human notion,
hovers a faithful Lover,
wed to the one who carries its song.

Only we can own
our Providence.
The entitlement is ours exclusively.

We bray: *if only I could find my purpose.*
To Creation, this sounds just like

a horse at river's edge,
whining for lack of water.

Purpose need not be found.
We never escape its presence.

What we need is a flashlight,
a torch of courage,
a daringness to project
our greatness across space,
to shred the dark into
a billion glints of revelation,

to thus behold the timid plant
that in the instance of our seeing,
transforms into a towering form.

A purposeful life must be lived
before it can become purpose.
It must be purposed before it can live.

This is no chicken and egg story.
This law is so old, it has lapped itself
in the currents of time.

Purpose lives in the waiting soil
of self-discovery,
is watered only when we dare
to believe that we were born
for a reason, then *leap* toward that reason.

Can't you hear the music
on the other side of the door?

The party started long ago.

You could be inside, and drunk
on a fulfilling life.

Instead, what you bring to the party
sits dormant in a tidy barrel
composed of your rings of fear.

You hold all the liquid light
required to reveal your truth.

You were born with the power
to erase darkness
and make the unseen visible.

Your barrel needs tilting,
then your freedom,

but first, you have to pour.

YOU RAISED ME

You raised me.

I was a corn stalk stalked by chaos,

supposed to be a towering edifice,
a pyramid, a monument to the sky,
but circumstance broke me down,
I don't know why.

I was crumbled
to grain to dust and dust again,
a sugar cane, soured in the shade,

a cherry tree sapling, bruised by hailstone,
a tender buttercup, my downside up,

and you raised me,
you praised me, you saved me,

you took me to the river
and dipped me down,
you cleansed me, washed me,
remade me.

You waited for me,
waited for my anger breathe,
waited for my fear to recede,
waited for my trust to sprout,
for my beauty to come out,
you waited for me.

You made it for me,
made my daily meal:
two slices of hope,
three laughs easy side over,
a glass of fresh squeezed joy,
and a warm bowl of healing,
high in fiber of nurturing.

You helped me sing, you found my thing
lost in the dust that chaos brings.

You led me to my song, at first
I sang it wrong, but you sat with me

while I practiced it. Soon, I grew so strong.

I learned my song, I earned my song,
I burned my early notes
in the fire you set for me,
and now I sing from memory,

I sing symphony, epiphany, destiny.

You lifted me,
you sifted me of all my sin,
you grifted my frown and gave me grin,
you hollowed out a treehouse space
where I could climb the vine of fantasy
and hang out in a crown of tree,

from there I look out across Vision Valley
and see all my future majesty...
you lifted me.

You prayed with me, you stayed with me
in the midnight hour, with candlelight
and cups of tea.

You helped me find my power,
looking out the window at bright full moon,
we found stars together that pointed the way
for what I was given life and breath to say,
what I was born to tell the world,

now, my flag unfurled, my rose uncurled,
my voice exposed, my pain transposed
into powerful clarity, I be the sweetest rarity.

You walk with me, you talk with me,
you listen when I share,
you show me a thousand silent ways
how much you care.

You bring me stories, your childhood allegories,
you bring the monsters out from under the bed
and hold them in your candlelight, so I can see
that monsters have no hold on me.

You wake with me,
you flake this stone with me,
this masterpiece I'm steady making,
you're never faking, always forsaking
the easier path, so I can swim in
Truth's hot and healing bath.

You shine me up, you line me up
and give me salutations, you honor me.

You raised me, you praised me,
you showed me what Love
looks like as it lives inside
a heart, a house, a childhood.

I wish you would now take a pause,
and receive this gift I bring to you.

I bring you my Sacred life,
lived on Purpose with a light not
conquered by hurtfulness.

I bring you my Sacred life,
evidence of what you poured faithfully,

You braised me, in your Loving sun,
your patient Loving hum,
the power of your Loving drum,
you braised me.

You raised me, you praised me,
you saved me, you slayed the shadows
and gave me light, you gave me life,
you gave me right, now I ascend,
majestic kite, I know my flight,
I have my target locked in sight:

A lifetime lived in a land called *Beautiful*.

I'm on my way, I'll get there soon,
and when you look to pregnant moon,
that smile you see looking back down
will be my Joy, and the light I shine
will simply be reflection of
all you were and are to me.

Whether we are side by side, or near or far,
remember, I am an always brightening star,
and that once and still...

You raised me.

THAT ONE MOMENT YOU GAVE

He ran into the young lady in the town center
while he was out with his daughters.

She ran up to him in a bolt,
swallowed him in a hug that bruised bones.

Tears made her face a delta,
sun rose from her mouth:

I just have to tell you
what you've done for me.

I teach reading and writing to homeless children
in a village in Nepal,

all because of a conversation you had with me
when I was a girl.

What did I say to you?

I was in a bad place in my life,
I had just thrown a fit,

you sat down with me,
said something that saved my life,

you said,
I believe all this pain will one day evaporate
and a beautiful soul will remain.

You will be fragrance
after the rain.

Children everywhere who secretly sorrow
will call you a true friend.

You said those words to me.
I remember each one clear as a crystal.

What you did not know was that
just before that conversation,
I was on my way to the park
to find somewhere soft and unseen
to lie down.

In my pocket, I had the pills.

I could no longer find anything
to hold onto to keep me in this world.
I had resolved to stop looking.

That one conversation with you,
your gentle, magic words,
made me want to live.

And you know those children I teach?
I tell them this story every time
I feel their surrender come near.

That one moment you gave me,
and the blessing you placed
inside that one moment,
lives on forever across the world from here,

in children you have never seen,
but have surely touched.

I just wanted you to know...
your giving made me want to live.

He lost all composure.
Their hug bruised all their bones.

Later, his daughters asked him,
daddy why were you crying
when that young lady was talking to you?

Because, my sweet dears,
her living made me want to give.

INFINITE HEART

Once, there lived a woman who had an infinite heart. Where suffering flared, she found it. Sat by it. Took its hand. Walked with it. Helped to build it up. She caught many tears in her caring palms. Listened to endless sorrow stories.

And always, she granted the suffering their dignity. She had faith and hope, which she shared like bread and water. She admired the lowest as the highest. She put the least first. She forever stood for truth and honor.

Others asked her, "How do you care so much? Don't you ever get burned out? Feel hopeless?"

She answered, "I am a social servant. Burnout and hopelessness are the divine gardens where I gratefully work. I am called by Sacredness to be a torch of compassion. As long as I drink from the endless reservoirs of Grace and Goodness, I have all that I need to serve every soul.

I learned long ago that when opened to the infinity of Love, a human heart becomes infinite. I am a social servant. Which is another title for one whose heart has lost its boundary, and gained Amazing Grace."

I CALL YOU LEGENDARY

For *all* those who serve children with honor:

They call you *social workers*,
but I drink my drinks from *Legend*,

so I recall a time
when family and community
were one and the same,

it was called a compound

and there were those people
of great sensitivity,

entrusted by the adults,
ratified by the elders to place their hands

upon the shoulders of children
and turn them to face a better wind.

They call you *social workers*.
I call you those who turn lives around.

You seep into cracks
like salvation blood and fill up the spaces
so precious little ones won't fall through.

They call you *social workers*...
I call you spirit keepers,
denizens of the light.
I mean to say, you reside
in a house called Hope
and keep the light on
so babies and lost folk
can find the way home.

They call you *social workers*,
but the ground you till is not social,
it is spiritual, *of the human spirit*,
it drips with black richness like strong coffee
picked from heaven's hills.

The seeds you protect are not simply children,
not simply tomorrow's daylight,
but the reason for our past,
and the purpose for our people to be,
to be.

I drink from *Legend*, so I know
mud-caked fishermen work the banks of the Nile
and have a faith that Creation will grace
them with good catch even on stingy days,
that they will be able to return home
to their families and fill bellies
with substance beyond yams...

this is your name.

And the griot,
she's old and over by the stump,
still got that reach,
even though her joints are stiff,
still got that reach to go on
and pull ripened fruit of symbolism
and legacy from the highest tree branches
and the most introverted clouds,

pickin' 'em and pickin' em,
and puttin' 'em in her story basket,
so that the young ones can fill their
minds with substance beyond what is,
extending out to what ought to be
and what used to be.

She just griot,
and she old,
but she young enough to set
young ones free.
This... is *your* name.

They call you social workers
in child welfare.

I call you medicine women and men
in family welfare.

I call you glue in the community
when rain come to pull things apart.

I call you doctors, priests, healers,

teachers, palm readers, fortune tellers,
prophesiers, negotiators, mediators,
advocators, instigators, pacifiers,
storytellers, truth dwellers,
getting downright dirty
in shameful cellars,
cleanin' up mess',
settin' crooked straight,

child soul caressers,
Man, Woman, I call you *masseuse*...

irrigators, investigators, neglect haters,
keeper of the cage that carries the canary
deep into the dark of human caves,
looking for that first sign of something foul,
praising that first sign of something beautiful...

And then there is this:
In a nation that says this community
is less than that one,
and this family is less than that one,
and this child is less than that one,
and why bother with all that pain,
they call you social workers who
go out and keep the faith.

Only one reason,
one reason be
so far as I can see:
Even the Blackest, Brownest, Whitest,
poorest, *brokest* community
is made up of beautiful
families and children
trying to get free,

each endowed with the full potential
of this Universe,
unshakable masterpieces of canvas untouched
by foolish nation using the wrong paintbrush,

and you...
in the morning when you rise,
you peel the frustration
from your sleepy face and eyes
and wash it away down the sink
with all that dirt *System* puts in your way,
and you walk clean out the door,

cause you believe.

You believe these children *are* good enough,
these families *are* worth enough,
these communities deserve enough,
and you absolutely have what it takes enough,
cause we don't ever make enough
money, material status, superficial dough,
to ever let it be okay to let some folk,
not even some kind of folk,
slip for just one day.

And I ask and I answer:
You *have* to be warriors,
cause you fought my battle,

you have to be magicians,
cause you carried me over wide water
with your barest feet,

you have to be the locksmith,
helping somebody who cared
for this little Black boy,
silent boy,
lost boy,

helping that somebody
turn the key and let me just be on my way
to being what I was put here to be.

And check this out:
Don't you *ever* think that
any one of these children could never
grow up to become legendary.

We are not the wisdom of Creation.

We occupy a more humble station
called imperfection,
and from this rippled surface
the distorted reflection we are able to catch,
is the Beauty of a day on down the path,
when the storm calms itself
and quits its crying.

Warped reflection
in the mirror of child welfare
is the child *fared well*,
is the day's bounty brought home
to somebody's hungry family,
to fill bellies with substance
beyond yams.

When I began this life,
you were there,

you carried me,
first to a safe way station,
then to my people who would
bring me up.

Child welfare,
or child farewell?

I put my money on the honey,
the sweet stuff, stories of success,
cause I am one,
cause you were one for me,
triumphant that is,
triumphant you were.

I am the reason
you get up and go out to work,
even in the bitter stretches
when fierce wind blows you back
and sharp sand stings your face...

you lean not backward,
you lean forward,

and I,
I can't just thank you,
that would be understatement.

I have to remind you of your
greatness, and how you leave
it in your wake so a child like me
can come 'round and lap it up
and taste some sweetness.

It tasted so good to me back then,
you want to know why? Because I,
I just wanted to be able to grow up
and have the chance to taste
some sweet potato pie.

I didn't want to slip through the cracks,
I didn't want to erode or fade away,
and I didn't want to die,
I just wanted to be able to grow up,
so I could have the chance to taste some
sweet potato pie,
cinnamon in my dreams,
fresh from the oven,
heavenly steam in my eye.

There is something called the system.
It is some parts working right
and some parts doing wrong,

but then there is the one who toils
for the well-being of the child,
you, made of flesh and of spirit,
some parts mad revolutionary,
calling for change when everything around
seems to just want to sit still,

some parts little child on the street corner
selling lemonade,
trying to make some coin
so she can get what she wants
to make the day feel good
in her hood.

And they,

lemme see now,
they...
call you social worker...

I call you Legendary.

I was one of the children.

Peace be deeply with you . . . .

CONTENTS

Jaiya John was born and raised in New Mexico, and has lived in various locations, including Nepal. He serves his life purpose through the blessings of faith, family, writing, speaking, and supporting young lives. He is the founder of Soul Water Rising, a global human mission. Jaiya gives truest thanks to the following:

Jacqueline V. Richmond and **Kent W. Mortensen** graciously and skillfully served as editors for *Legendary*. **Arturo Aviña** was also a valuable editing contributor.

•

Titles available through booksellers everywhere. Revenue from Soul Water Rising titles and speaking services funds our *Young Life Drumbeat* youth development programming.

Other Books by Jaiya John

To learn more about this and other books by Jaiya John, to order discounted bulk quantities, or to learn about Soul Water Rising's global work, please visit us at:

soulwater.org

jaiyajohn.com

facebook.com/jaiyajohn

youtube.com/soulwaterrising

itunes (jaiya john)

To subscribe for free to our life enrichment e-journal, *SOUL BLOSSOM*, please visit soulwater.org.

Soul Blossom is part newsletter. Park creative space. Entirely renewing your soul. Offering ongoing news of our global human mission; new book release notices; speaking engagement insights; and invited literary contributions from notable individuals.

Soul Blossom is also a gathering space for the writing and artwork of young people from around the world.

•

To subscribe for free to *FRESH PEACE: DAILY EMAIL INSPIRATIONS*, please visit soulwater.org.

Fresh Peace offers daily reflections and stories to lift your spirit, brighten your day, and renew your life. A weekly subscription is also available.

CPSIA information can be obtained at www.ICGtesting.com
Printed in the USA
LVOW12s1719261214

420469LV00001B/1/P